Introduction to
AFRICAN ART

Introduction to
AFRICAN ART

Boris de Rachewiltz

TRANSLATED BY
PETER WHIGHAM

JOHN MURRAY

TO MARY

CONTENTS

ILLUSTRATIONS

Illustrations

Illustrations

xi

Illustrations

Illustrations

xiii

Illustrations

xiv

Illustrations

Illustrations

AUTHOR'S NOTE

I would like to thank the following institutions and individuals for the help which they have extended to me in the course of the preparation of this book: members of the Frobenius Institute at Frankfurt-on-Main; Professor Dr Ad. E. Jensen; Dr H. Klein; Dr E. Haberland; the Curator of the Museum für Völkerkunde at Munich; Dr O. Zerries; Mr C. A. Burland, E.O. of the British Museum; and Dr Fabrizio Mori for providing the reports of his expeditions to the Fezzan and allowing the reproduction of some of the illustrations hitherto unpublished. Grateful acknowledgements are also due to the following collections and collectors, public and private: Dr L. Segy of the Segy Gallery of New York; M. Charles Ratton of Paris; Mr C. Kjersmeier of Copenhagen; Casa Coray of Agnuzzo, Lugano; Herr Kofler-Truniger of Lucerne; and in Milan, Dr R. Jucker; Professor O. Da Re; Professor E. Bozzi; Baron A. von Hoerschelmann, all of whom have kindly allowed the author to reproduce various pieces from their collections. I am similarly indebted to Raffaele Carrieri for valuable information about the *avant-garde* in art, on which he is an authority; to Giovanni and Vanni Scheiwiller; to the painter G. L. Giovanola; to the Nigerian sculptor L. Wadiri; and to Mr E. Walrond for invaluable assistance from London. Finally, to the l'Istituto Italiano per l'Africa, where I was able to make various useful contacts on the occasion of the Institute's International Congress of Negro writers and artists. I would particularly like to thank Dr Quirino Maffi for his friendly assistance.

The origin of each picture is indicated in the caption. I have personally selected the reproductions of the unpublished pieces from private collections and Institutions. The golden Wallace mask is reproduced with permission of the Curator of the Wallace Collection. Dr L. Segy, Charles

Author's Note

Ratton and Kofler-Truniger have been responsible for taking photographs of the pieces from their collections.

The English translation has been made in close collaboration between the translator and myself.

INTRODUCTION

Europe's introduction to African art was an adjunct to the artistic revolution that took place at the beginning of this century: it was not the work of specialists. Everywhere, artists were in revolt against nineteenth-century academicism. All accepted values were in question. In this situation, artists such as Picasso, Matisse, Brancusi, Modigliani, Gaudier-Brzeska and many others, turned to African art as a fresh and vital source of inspiration. The effect, however, which this art had on them is confined to that of plastic form, filtered through the sensibility of the individual artist. It was valued for its own sake and was submitted to the artist's subjective and purely aesthetic interpretation.

This was a mistaken approach—although a fruitful one: the objects which European artists regarded as works of art had not been conceived as such by their creators. The African craftsman, or 'artist', breathed life into a particular form, or limited himself to the repetition of certain traditional themes for reasons which were in no sense 'artistic'. To understand these reasons, and the purpose of the objects produced, it is necessary to place oneself in the psychological context of the civilisations of which they form a part. They must be viewed in the conceptual framework which generated them. To explain that framework is the purpose of this book.

There are two secondary themes. First, the impact of Africa on modern art has itself been so considerable that it demands special treatment in a study of this kind. Hence, the book includes an examination of this impact, together with a survey of the works of those European artists who obviously owe most to it. Second, as a matter of immediate and pressing interest, the future of Negro art is also touched on.

Introduction

To deprive a people of their inner motives for producing works of art is to subject them to the severest psychological trauma. This is what colonialism has done to the people who comprise the civilisations of Black Africa. What can they be expected to retain of their former, age-old sensibilities? In what direction is any new art likely to develop? Where are they most likely to look for inspiration? These questions can only be answered by an investigation of the artistic activities of the contemporary Negro. Thus the influence of African art on modern European art, and the future of Negro art, both grow out of the main subject of the book, which is the immensely ancient legacy bequeathed to us by the Black Continent.

There is a tendency in books on this subject to fail to distinguish the quality of the work they include. Productions typical of some important school, or stylistic centre, are placed side by side with the inferior productions of third-rate craftsmen. This is curious, for in any other sort of art criticism, whether old or new, Oriental or European, it is customary to take into account only the work of masters and of the schools they founded: that of contemporary dilettantes, or dabblers, is ignored. In the case of African art, its very nature precludes the attribution of particular works to particular artists. It is, however, perfectly possible to distinguish between the work of a master craftsman, or his school, and of that which, at best, possesses little except a doubtful ethnographic interest. Thus in the present work only the best examples in the various fields have been included. Although the criterion of selection has been technical—certain exceptions being made for purposes of comparison—the author believes that the essential characteristics of African art have been preserved. It is, indeed, his hope that by means of this innovation the reader may arrive at a more complete understanding of the works concerned, and, as a result, at a deeper knowledge of the Negro mind.

1

THE SETTING AND
THE ACTORS

Africa is a black diamond whose thousand facets reflect a thousand different scenes. She is Africa *portentosa*, 'mother of marvels' as the early explorers called her. Her eleven million square miles comprise the fertile Mediterranean region, steppe, savannah, parching desert, and dense equatorial forests. Landscape and climate undergo drastic revolutions; environmental conditions alter, and with them vegetation, animal life and racial types. Great rivers, broken every now and then by huge waterfalls, unwind themselves through limitless distances. Mountains, capped with eternal snows, are reflected in great lakes of which one, Victoria, is the size of Switzerland. The atmosphere is charged with primordial energy. It is as though one could overhear the deep breathing of creative forces, still at work, taking their primaeval shapes. In the depths of petrified forests archaic forms of life defy the slow flow of thousands of years. Recently, a fish thought to be long extinct was discovered in the Zambesi. It has lungs and the rudiments of limbs. It is a transitional link occupying the same position in the zoological chain as our ancestors of the Devonian period, who lived millions of years ago, and of whom to-day no trace remains, except for a few fossilised relics.

Evidence of the existence in Africa of the earliest human types, the subhuman forerunners of *homo sapiens*, dating from the Pleistocene period, is to be found in the pre-hominid Australopithecines of South Africa. The various stages through which primitive man has passed are marked first by Africanthropus, then by Rabat man, Diré-Daua man, Rhodesian man, Boskop man, Mechta el-Arbi man,

1

and Asselar man. Among these types we can observe points of contact with the Cro-Magnon and Grimaldi stock. Moreover, the pictures and rock engravings which decorate the great wall galleries of North-West Africa, the Sahara, the Libyan and Nubian deserts and South Africa, are clearly related to similar Franco-Cantabrian works, and to the cave drawings in Eastern Spain.

In Europe, however, the dynamics of environmental change have been such as to effect profound physiological changes in man himself. Agriculture was practised early and soon rationalised; there have been migrations, wars, invasions, conquests and widely spread trading operations. In Africa the picture is quite different. Here, civilisations have indeed risen and declined, and there have been migrations and internal wars; but the pervasive effect of all-powerful natural forces, together with the isolation imposed upon a people still living within an archaic cycle, have preserved intact, into the present day, a cast of mind surviving from the remotest ages. Africans are mentally oriented to a world of magic, of omnipresent and invisible forces no less real to them than the objects of everyday life.

In the same way as the fish has preserved its morphological identity over millions of years, so we can trace in to-day's cosmological beliefs, in ritual practices and collective customs, survivals of that world of thought which typifies the most ancient of African civilisations. The survivals are for the most part decadent in comparison with the original cycles. And this is particularly true where theocracies have degenerated into low forms of witchcraft, which occurred even without the disintegrating aid of colonialism. The tendency of scholars to form judgements on the basis of these degenerate forms is the result of widespread fallacies—intellectual idols, in the Baconian sense—which it is necessary to destroy. The most vicious of these is the meaning given to the term 'primitive', applied indiscriminately to different types of people and their ways of life. The abuse of this term has been, and still is, a source of considerable error and confusion.

The Setting and the Actors

Etymologically, 'primitive' means an initial state. In ethnography it is applied to human beings whose physiognomy is primaeval, indicating that they live in 'pre-civilised' conditions and are of 'pre-logical' mentality. Clearly such terminology has its uses and can be justified in certain cases. It should not, however, be abused, which is what happens when it is used, facilely, as a label to distinguish manifestations of thought and belief which differ from those of the self-styled 'rational' person who applies it. A serious scientific analysis cannot be content with approximations: it must insist on the closest correlation of word to object.

In relation to Africa, the term 'primitive' seems singularly inappropriate. It is not possible to limit one's enquiries to the situation as it is to-day. This would be to treat the conditions to which the majority of the population has been reduced, both through internal and, more particularly, external causes, as though they had existed *ab origine* and been, as it were, arrested in some sort of stasis. In point of fact, when we turn to inspect the evidence of past periods, there is eloquent testimony of the presence of flourishing civilisations where to-day a few herdsmen survey their scant pastures.

The vanished civilisation of Nok, which is usually attributed to the middle of the first millennium BC, and which was recently brought to light by the excavations of Bernard Fagg; the fabulous empires of Ghana and of Sosso; the Empire of Mosi and Mali; the Ife civilisation, and the Kingdom of Benin, are only a memory to-day kept alive by pieces treasured in museums and private collections; but these amply attest the former splendour of these cultures, as they do the degree of artistic evolution which they attained. In the variety of African civilisations it is possible to discern examples of morphological beginnings, moments of interaction, the climax of a civilisation, and its decadence. To apply to all this, as well as to the crepuscular psychological forms, involute and retrograde in nature, the single term 'primitive', is a fundamental error of

3

method. There is of course Carl Einstein's aphorism: 'Primitivism in art is equally a beginning or an end.' But in the commonly accepted use of the phrase, that is, as meaning the *terminus a quo*, or initial stage of a process, its use in this context is inadmissible. It is a hallmark of ignorance. In the early days of colonialism, when missionaries and slave-traders were our sole sources of information, there may have been some slight justification for it. To-day there is none.

To revert to the world of magic: it has already been said that by most Africans, material reality and spirit are not conceived of as separate existences. On the contrary, everything is felt to be in a state of cohesion, of unity, as if the cosmos were a sea of fluid forces perpetually vibrating and manifesting themselves in particular times and places, and in specific ways, of which material manifestation is only one. An African feels he is immersed in this sea of forces, and that he shares their vitality, not so much as an individual but as a group. His *ego* has not been submitted to the synthesis of individualism brought to bear by other civilisations. It exists in a fluid state which enables it to absorb itself into the group. This sense of collectivity induces a mental attitude which makes itself apparent in every circumstance of life. It is the basis of an African's code of ethics, and an action will be judged good or evil according to the effect it has on the group.

The dialogue: 'The world and I', is thus the product of many voices. There are the other members of the clan, and the voices of the communal-blood-ancestor—who may also have a totem aspect; and these are fused into a single unit. This is the origin of the idea of participation: 'the whole having the character of the parts and the parts of the whole'. To be a member of a group is like forming a link in a magnetic chain: so long as contact is maintained, the individual shares in the power generated by the group as a whole. For the individual to break the link, to become separate from the chain, spells death, and not merely moral death. It is therefore necessary to seal the psyche indelibly with the impress of those ties which unite the individual to the group. The initiation ceremonies by which this is achieved are highly dramatic, and are equivalent to the voluntary death of the individual and his rebirth into the collective life of the tribe.

At this point it is necessary to outline the essential nature of these rites; for many of the objects which European aesthetic sensibility has classified as 'works of art' are in fact ritual instruments, strictly functional in purpose. The candidates prepare for the initiation ceremony by a period of separation from their families. They are herded together in an isolated place where they are instructed in the traditions of the tribe, in the laws that regulate communal life, and in matters affecting procreation. Frequent recourse is made to ancestral communion. The blessing of the dead is invoked to strengthen the ties uniting the individual candidates with the tribal forefathers. The youths are made to undergo severe physical tests, which they endure in a spirit of emulation, re-enacting the warlike virtues of their tribal past, the deeds of heroism, and the sufferings that have been handed down to them in oral tradition. A special diet accompanies this period of preparation and purification.

When the day dawns, the candidates stimulate themselves by means of frenzied dances whose movements are calculated to induce a state of ecstasy. It is at this point, among many tribes, that the mask assumes its essential function. By covering the features of the individual, already disposed to hyper-consciousness, it acts as a sort of dynamo to this state and enables the vital process of transformation to take place. In the Congo, in Bapende initiation rites, the *minyaki* mask represents the life of adolescence which is being left behind, and the act of stripping it off and discarding it, which is performed during the ceremony, is more than a symbolic gesture. The powers inherent in the mask itself invest it with magic force. Dramatically it represents the catharsis and palingenesis which generates the 'new birth': it is the individual 'ἐκπύρωσις that both

5

dissolves and coagulates. This is why the Mendi, in Sierra Leone, use a mask representing a demon that first swallows and then vomits the candidate whose head has been carefully shaved in order to mimic the appearance of a new-born child. The childish pigtail pinned to the candidate's head in Pharaonic Egypt had the same significance.

Other tribes, instead of wearing masks, daub their bodies with kaolin which they apply in accordance with tribal symbolism. However, the climax and epitome of these ceremonies is provided by the act of circumcision, which contains in itself all the essential qualities of a *rite de passage*. The forms taken by this ritual vary from tribe to tribe. Among the Mahalbi, between the Niger and Lake Chad, they are startlingly dramatic. In fact what takes place is not so much an act of circumcision, as the infliction of wounds, *in locis genitalibus*, by a strange creature in the guise of a leopard, who unexpectedly pounces on the youths from the cover of the bush.

In other regions, the initiator wears a terrifying mask, intended to heighten the dramatic impact of this part of the rite, and so deepen the suffering which it entails. This in its turn, by stirring into life psychic relationships hitherto unacknowledged, and by dynamising the candidate's latent spiritual forces, will effect the desired act of individual metamorphosis. The candidate's childhood clothes are burnt, and he receives a new name from his godfather, ratifying his changed state. In the name is the essence: this is a conception that links Africa to other cycles of ancient civilisations, and which assumes particular importance in Pharaonic Egypt. In the coronation ritual, which was specifically initiatory in character, the Pharaoh was given a new royal title that superseded all his other titles, and was conveyed to him in an elliptical cartouche symbolising solar power.

On initiation, the individual enters into full tribal life and becomes eligible for various tribal positions. The elders bless the young man's assumption into society with suitable formulas. The Kikuyu employ an invocation to peace:

'May peace be with our children. May God grant us peace. May peace be with our children, peace.'

Similar initiation rites are prescribed for women, but they take place separately from those for the men. With women also, a period of preparation and purification precedes the actual ceremony. The instruction which they receive in the isolation period turns largely on the young girls' future roles as wives and mothers and is basically concerned with sexual matters, with procreation, the upbringing of children and domestic management. Among the Kikuyu they bathe in the river, holding above their heads a sacred branch whose leaves they scatter on the water as a symbol of the attitudes and desires of childhood which they have put behind them. This ceremony is similar to the rite performed by the *Bakhimbu* secret society in the Mayombe region of the Congo, in which the candidates are immersed in the water in order, symbolically, to wash away their past lives. In the *Bakhimbu*, at the same moment as being given their new name, the candidates are also given sacred food to eat as a sacramental link between what they were and what they are about to become. The food is said to contain *nyama*, or vital energy. Female circumcision is by no means uniform among all tribes, although it generally consists of the practice of clitoridectomy, the ritual being performed by an old woman who has specialised in the operation.

The specifically sexual character of initiation ceremonies, whether male or female, underlines the emphasis which all African societies place on procreation and fertility. More than this, a study of the original conceptions which are expressed in these rites, leads to the discovery of other associated values. Among the Dogon of the French Sudan, the male and female principles are held to coexist in each individual at the moment of birth. Anatomically, the female principle in a man is represented by the prepuce, and that of the male in a woman by the clitoris. It follows that the act of initiation, with the circumcision rite proper to it, takes the form of a definitive confirmation of the individual's sex; it is the sign that he or she should now be

7

considered as a fully adult male or female. This explains why the Dogon have produced a specifically hermaphroditic type of statuary, as indeed have many other African tribes. The Ashanti call the male principle transmitted through the paternal line, *ntoro*, and the female principle transmitted through the maternal line, *abusua*. Both principles are believed to co-exist in every human being. *Ntoro*, as the source of strength and fertility, is the object of a special cult. Offerings to *ntoro* are placed in a sacred vessel, the *kuduo*, which I shall describe when we come to the subject of Ashanti bronzes.

It is customary, during the initiation ceremony, for tattooings and scarifications to be executed on the candidate. The skin is cut, and vegetable ash or sap is rubbed into the wound, so that the scars stand out in relief and form a decorative pattern. This pattern, which is sometimes of a complex symbolism, constitutes the tribe's 'mark' by which members can identify each other, and from which they derive the pride of belonging to a distinct group. The same sense of pride shows itself in the tribal name, which normally embodies the notion of 'man' *par excellence*. Thus *Bantu* means 'men'; *Warega* means 'everybody', or 'humanity'; *Hottentot*, 'all the people'; *Zulu*, 'the people'; *Bayaka*, 'males'; *Babali*, 'we' and 'the people'; *Wagogo*, 'those with heads'; *Yalnas*, 'sons of men'; *Balendu*, 'the race itself'; *Sao*, 'men'. It would be possible to give numerous other examples. The importance of this ethnocentralism lies in the dignity it attributes to the tribal element, *per se*. It is an attitude which reminds one—at least on the idealogical level—of the innate superiority felt by 'civilised' races when confronted with other nations.

As well as the initiation rituals of which we have been speaking, and which constitute the *sine qua non* of tribal life, there are also ceremonies designed for the admission of adults into secret societies. Here there are notable points of contact with the old initiations into the Mysteries of classical antiquity. In many instances these organisations have degenerated into little more than political sects; but they wield great influence, and possess absolute power of life and death over their members. In such organisations the mask is once again of fundamental importance. It may act as an agent of psychological change; or it may be used as a symbol of rank and power. These particular forms of association will be considered more fully in the section which deals with the mask.

Above all, the African's religious instincts express themselves in ancestor worship; that is, in rites aimed at establishing and maintaining communion with the founders of the tribe. The concept is purely terrestrial, not to say material: there is no thought of spirits inhabiting a separate 'Paradise', but rather of beings who are a part of the material order of this world and who, though invisible, are still subject to certain of its physical laws. We even find that they require nourishment, and, as a result, food offerings form an important part of burial ceremonies, as was once the case in ancient Egypt. The custom of making a 'double' of the dead person, in the form of a statuette, is yet another example of the substrate of thought shared by African and Nilotic cultures.

The actual manufacture of the statues is a matter of ritual, the result of precise techniques evolved by the witch-doctor. These principally consist of charging the statue with *nyama*, or vital energy, to enable it to establish contact with other levels of existence. This is a far remove from the creation of *objets d'art* aimed at the stimulation of aesthetic feeling.

Originally, the Portuguese coined the term 'fetish' from *feitiço*, meaning 'that which is false', or the result of witchcraft. They applied it to Negro statuary, dogmatically asserting that African cults were exclusively fetishistic, consisting of the worship of statues and inanimate objects. Such a theory has been quite rightly denounced by Carl Einstein, who writes: 'African statues are often called fetishes: everyone uses the word; but it explains nothing, and can mean whatever you want it to mean. It conceals both the significance of the sculpture and our own ignorance of that significance. The perfectly clear intention of the objects is lost sight of under a weight of terminology.' And Frobenius explicitly asserts that he himself has never encountered fetishism in any part of Africa. This theme will be developed more fully, when we come to statuary. What is important at the moment is to dispel certain deep-seated prejudices and *idées fixes*.

As has been said, true tribal religion takes the form of ancestor worship. There is no cult of a Supreme Being, with a body of ritual centred solely on him, to be found in any African civilisation. To an African, the Supreme Being is, by nature, such that he does not require worship: a cult devoted to his honour would be necessarily useless. An African's concept of God is essentially monotheistic; his name varies among different tribes, and his attitude to his creation is held to be one of complete indifference. An Archecho witch-doctor will tell you: 'God is everywhere; he is in the air we breathe. He is no one form, but he permeates the entire world.' The anthropomorphic and omnipresent Deity whom the Kikuyu call *Ngai* is invoked on only four occasions, each of climacteric importance, in an individual's life: that is, at birth, initiation, marriage and death. Only at these times is communication sought with him as well as with the ancestral spirits. On other occasions, contact is the result of collective rather than individual need. According to Jomo Kenyatta, the Kikuyu have a saying: 'God lives in the sky; he is not concerned with one man's business, but with the business of the whole race, or the clan. There is no cult or sacrifice that will avail for one man alone.' And they have another saying: 'There is no point in bothering *Ngai*!'

The Ewe of Togo call the Supreme Being, *Mawu*, while the Dualas of the Cameroons refer to him as *Nyambe*; both these groups consider it unnecessary to address sacrifices to him, preferring the worship of ancestral spirits and other natural forces more readily accessible than an incommensurable godhead. The very closeness of these forces to the earth, their materiality, means that they are more likely to be affected by men's actions, good or bad. Such beliefs favour the development of a naturalistic religion, which does not preclude the concept of a Supreme Being, but does mean that, except on rare occasions, he is not the object of direct worship. The exceptions to this principal, provided, for instance, by the Mofus of the Cameroons and the Batongo, are examples of personification rather than of the anthropomorphism with which we started, the one identifying God with the sky, and the other with the earth.

The Supreme Being is invoked in the council of elders, both for spiritual guidance, and on behalf of the well-being of the community. Among the Kikuyu, one of the elders recites the alternate lines of the following invocation, while the council utters the refrain, thus:

> Give light to the elders; let them speak with one voice.
> *Praise be to Ngai. Peace be with us.*
> Give the country peace; let the people increase.
> *Praise be to Ngai. Peace be with us.*
> Give the race prosperity, and their flocks and herds; let them be free of sickness.
> *Praise be to Ngai. Peace be with us.*
> Give the fields fruitful harvest; let the land be fertile.
> *Praise be to Ngai. Peace be with us.*

The chiefs and kings act as intermediaries between the people and the world of the gods and are consequently invested with divine authority. They sometimes fill the role of scapegoats in expiation of the collective sins of the tribe, whose welfare depends on their own.* This is the

* There was a special rite among the Ashanti to sustain the vital ties connecting the king and his people. Every Thursday, attended by his followers and the members of his family, the king visited a part of his palace called *akrafieso*, or 'House of Spirits'. There he filled his mouth with holy water from a ritual gold vessel called *akra yewan*, 'Cup of Spirits', and then spat it around him, saying: 'Life for me: health for my people!'

In ancient Egypt, the Pharaoh conducted a similar rite in the sacred recess called *Per Dwat*, or 'House of Heaven', pronouncing the following formula: 'Holy spirits of Heliopolis, you and I depend for our safety on each other. Your *Ka* is safe if my *Ka*—the first of all living *Ka* (the people) —is safe. All live if I live. . . .' After which, the people in acknowledgement of the bond uniting them to him, say: 'My *Ka* belongs to the king, my *Ka* comes from the king, the king makes my *Ka*, the king is my *Ka*. . . .'

It was on the basis of this mutual dependence that all ancient theocracies were founded.

explanation of the ritual sacrifice of the king, practised until quite recently among the Dagombas of Togo and the Mbous of the Cameroons. It consisted of his being violently done away with at the first signs of physical decrepitude. If it is assumed that the people's well-being is intimately connected with the condition of the sovereign, not only on the moral plane, but physically, on account of his nature as a mediating vessel, then it follows that a falling away of his powers will be attended by a comparable decline in the people as a whole and, ultimately, by their ruin.

Other ancient civilisations share the same conceptions, and sacrifice not only the king, but his wives and slaves as well, in order that he may be properly attended in the next world. The discoveries at Sakkara show this to have been the case in Egypt, in the earliest historical period; while the Kushite people of Kerma provide more recent evidence of similar practices.

On such a level of civilisation as this, every object has its special function: whether it be a mask, a statue, or a rock painting, it will have been created with a precise end in view. The object can be thought of as a husk or shell: it contains vital force. But it is at the same time the force itself—if it has been constructed in accordance with the correct magic formulas. For it is precisely an object's external form that determines its evocative power. By means of heightened consciousness man attains a union with the forces that are evoked: he becomes identified with cosmic rhythms manifesting themselves at levels other than his own.

Here then is the setting in which we are to look at the various civilisations of Africa—and these are the actors.

1. Rhinoceros. Rock *graffito* of the earliest cycle. 10 ft. 8 ins. × 5 ft. Acacus Massif, Fezzan.

2. Two men. Rock painting. 7 ins. × 10½ ins. Kargur, Libya.

3. Schematised animals. Polychrome rock painting (in yellow, white, brown and black). 3 ft. 6 ins. ×7 ft. 4 ins. Matopo Hills, Modschelele, Rhodesia.

4. Winged monster. Rock painting. 10½ ins. × 1 ft. 1¾ ins.

5. Centaur. Rock painting. 9 ins. × 11 ins. Umtali, Penhalonga, Rhodesia.

6. Head of a man in terracotta. Height 9 ins. Jemaa,
N. Nigeria.

7. Terracotta probably representing the usurper Lajuwa.
Original life-size. Ife, S. Nigeria.

8. Woman's head in terracotta, discovered by Leo Frobenius at Ife. Height 8 ins.

9. A modern cast of a bronze head, made by the 'cire perdue'
method. Yoruba.

2

THE ROCK WORKS

Easily the oldest evidence of 'artistic' activity to be found in the Black Continent, whether in the form of *graffiti* or paintings, are the rock works. Those in the North African Maghreb are commonly ascribed to the Capsian, neolithic epoch; while radio-carbon tests performed in the remains at Él Mekhta, and at Dra Mta el-Abiod in Algeria, have yielded dates of approximately 6650 and 5050 BC, respectively. The Abbé Breuil estimated that the earliest South African figures are 10,000 years old, though van Riet Lowe and Schofield prefer a somewhat later date. What is beyond question, in all the works with which we are acquainted— particularly those of North Africa—is that thousands of years before our era African artists were entrusting to their rock walls, in the deserts or in caves, the results of their pictorial experience, and for very much the same reasons as inspired our own prehistoric artists who produced the remarkable Franco-Cantabrian and Eastern Spanish work.

We are already in the world of magic, for it is the principles of imitative magic that lie at the root of the rock figures, the belief being that there is the closest connection —a mystic union—between an object and its representation. The drawn line creates a form. The closer the resemblance between the form and its corresponding reality, the stronger the bond between them. This is the basis of naturalism in art. On the other hand, stylised and progressively abstract forms tend to undermine the correspondence between form and object by making a generality of the object's individual properties.

When the individual characteristics that bind the figure to a specific object have been eliminated, the artist is left with a radical archetypal element: an ideal human or animal prototype. Thus the dialogue 'the world and I' is refashioned by the artist under the twin impulses of fear and self-preservation. The 'world' here is nature, a nature that will not accept man's domination, and is the primitive nomadic hunter's constant enemy. Wild beasts of every sort lie perpetually in ambush—from huge mastodons whose mere size is a source of terror, to the smallest animals whose lethal poisons are even more terrifying. And then there are the encroachments of warlike neighbours, with the fighting and skirmishes that ensue. Fluid consciousness 'sees' these natural forces in personified forms by dramatising their appearances. Besides wild beasts, one meets zoocephallic and anthropomorphic creatures, ghosts and spectres. This 'world' is plainly antagonistic to the individual who is forced to develop within himself his own means of holding it at bay. Consciousness, still fluid and not yet crystallised in rational patterns of thought, provides the ambience in which intuitive introspection can prompt the elements of the magic dialogue.

In this there is no difference between prehistoric Africa and prehistoric Europe, except that in Europe the dialogue has been discontinued, while in Africa it can be heard to-day, even though in the degenerate forms of 'magic' and 'witchcraft'. In this connection, Paul Germann's discoveries among the Gissi, those of Leo Frobenius in the Hombori Mountains, and of Desplagnes in the bend of the Niger, are of the highest significance. Here, to this day, a clay wall is erected during public initiation ceremonies, on which the candidates are made to copy figures of ancient prototypes, while at the same time giving free rein to their fantasy. In front of this wall, moreover, they deposit certain clay puppets. The perpetuation of such practices into modern times has induced some students to believe that all rock works of this sort may be of recent execution: an opinion that has been proved to be untenable. For many of the rock works show that what are now dry regions of scorching desert were once fertile plains where herds of cattle found abundant grazing. Not only that, but the animal life depicted in them is often either extinct or has moved out of the region and further south. This has been the case with the *Bubalus antiquus*, the elephant, the hippopotamus, the rhinoceros and the crocodile, all of which are reproduced on the rock walls of the Atlas Mountains. This in itself is a great help in dating such works.

In outline, the areas in which African rock art developed are as follows:

North Africa:
A. the Maghreb, the Atlas Mountains (with regions of special density in Hoggar, Tassili, Fezzan, Aïr, Tibesti, In Ezzan); Egypt and Libya.

Equatorial Africa:
A. Abyssinia and the former Anglo-Egyptian Sudan;
B. Nigeria;
C. the Cameroons;
D. Katanga, Angola.

East Africa:
A. Tanganyika.

South Africa:
A. Rhodesia, The Orange Free State, Drakensburg (Natal), the Transvaal, The Cape region.

While keeping within the limits of a general survey, let us examine the outstanding features of the works found in these areas.

The works of the Atlas Mountains have been classified by Frobenius and Obermaier according to style and technique as follows:

Group 1: Prehistoric engravings (the line deeply incised)
      A. naturalistic style;
      B. semi-naturalistic style.

Introduction to African Art

Group 2: *Libyan-Berber engravings* (chiselled pointillism)
    A. naturalistic style;
    B. semi-naturalistic style.

Group 3: *Arabic engravings and modern graffiti.*

It will be observed, first, that this classification is confined to the engravings and does not include the paintings; and that, second, its main aim technically is to distinguish between engraving in depth (characteristic of the oldest period), and the technique whereby the line is obtained by chiselling the wall surface in a pointillist fashion. Furthermore as the works were all executed in the open they have been subjected to effects of weathering, and these have created patinas that help considerably in dating.

It is, however, the ecology of the subject that is of most value for this purpose. In the first period the long-horned buffalo, to-day extinct, appears amid humid-tropical vegetation. There are elephants, rhinoceri, giraffes and (in the Auenat Massif) okapi. There are human figures in the form of hunters, at first armed with bows, and later with javelins and short stabbing swords. There follow figures of domestic animals such as oxen, sheep and asses. The last two periods show the domestic horse, which was introduced into the Sahara about 1500 BC, and the camel, introduced between the third and sixth centuries BC.

In the Fezzan, in the Western Sahara and in Wadi Gerat there are engravings and paintings of carriages that reveal Mediterranean penetration. The attitudes of the horses, and the 'flying gallop' typical of Mycenaean art, indicate the origin of such penetration and the probable period at which it took place. In my book on Egyptian art I have discussed the use of the 'flying gallop' on the tombs of Ancient Egypt, and demonstrated the evident Aegean influence on Nilotic art of the period of Amenhotep III.

Paolo Graziosi, a leading authority on the prehistoric Sahara, considers it possible that the substrate of successive artistic developments throughout the Mediterranean region may have had its origin in the Spanish rock figures:

'elements of it [this art] seem to manifest themselves in the productions of some of the older arts such as the Egyptian and Minoan'.

The scenes on the rock walls of the Fezzan are, above all, of animals. There are examples of former species of buffaloes, and of elephants and rhinoceri. These are mostly shown in the act of charging, as at Tel Issaghen and In

Drawing 1. Man seated. Rock *graffito*. 1 ft. × 8 ins.
Wadi in Habeter, Fezzan.

Habeter. The pictures of giraffes and ostriches inside magical circles are intended to secure success in the hunt. An emotive connection was held to exist between the power of the image and objective reality, and in this connection lay the possibility of homeopathic action. The style of these works is for the most part highly expressive and naturalistic, though there is also a tendency to stylisation and abstraction, as in the case of the human figure copied by Frobenius at In Habeter (Drawing 1). The elegantly linear sketches of giraffes and ostriches (Drawing 2) display exceptionally bold craftsmanship and appear to be the result of accomplished maturity. There are also sacred animals such as the goat with the disk between its horns, which Schwinfurth connected with similar animals in

Ancient Egypt, holy to Ammon. Disks and spirals between the horns are met with in other animals such as oxen, antelope and hippopotami.

To the Arabs, the rock pictures are *hajra mektuba,* 'the written stones', and are the subject of strange traditions and legends. In the Fezzan, for instance, where the Kingdom of the Garamanti, described by Herodotus, flourished

Drawing 2. Giraffe. Rock *graffito*. 8 ins. × 4 ins.
Wadi in Habeter, Fezzan.

2,000 years ago, mysterious figures are said to rise from the rocks and, transfixing the unwary traveller with their look, turn him to stone. Corresponding ideas are to be found in the Lake Chad region.

The paintings were executed in the shelter of caves, better suited to the rites of witchcraft than were rocky terraces beaten by the sun. The range of colours comprised red ochre, light yellow, blue, and black and white. With these, on the roughly smoothed cave walls, the artist invested his pictures, in either isolated or grouped compositions, with a splendid vitality. As with the engravings, there is the nomadic hunting period and the pastoral period, and ecology provides a useful chronological guide. In the same caves there are paintings of later periods, and even of quite recent times, for the Tuareg appear occasionally to use the cave walls for decorative purposes. The human figures in the oldest pictures are naked; later they appear clothed in the shape of a double triangle or bell.

The subjects are magical. They refer to fertility rites; and in these there are signs of sexual practices some of which are still to be found in parts of Africa. There are rites to promote successful hunting expeditions, to bring good fortune in war, and to produce rain; the pictures are composed of anthropomorphic and zoomorphic figures. In some instances masked men appear to be engaged in ritual or hunting activities; in others, beings with human bodies are portrayed with animal heads. Such appearances are obviously perceived as absolutely real by the minds of those who painted them. The real presence of similar beings, usually considered harmful to humans, is still firmly believed by many African peoples, so much so that special amulets are made to avert chance encounters with them.

The caves of In Ezzan, of Wadi Gerat and Wadi Mertutek, all contain important paintings, although it would be more accurate to describe those in Wadi Mertutek as being not so much in 'caves' as in natural cavities under the rocks, varying in height from 5,900 to 6,800 feet. They comprise figures of oxen with their drovers, and of the celebrated 'dancers' which are reproduced in almost all the illustrations of the rock works.

It is in this area of the Sahara, the Fezzan, that Fabrizio Mori has recently made a series of discoveries of exceptional interest. He began his expeditions in 1955, and the documentation he has since assembled is of the highest value from its quantity as well as quality.

Near Wadi Ekki, in the Ghat region, hunting scenes and masked dances form the subject of the rock pictures. Mori has recognised in one crouching figure a very strong Egyptian influence which, in my opinion, is probably the result of one of those recurrent cultural waves which we know took place in the still uncharted period of Saharan and Nilotic prehistory. In the same region, a series of rock incisions centred on the Acacus Massif depict ritual coupling in order to promote fertility. The male figures are masked while the women are represented in all the elegance of elaborate *parures*. There is an ithyphallic, anthropomorphic being with a zoomorphic mask; it is shown in a frontal position and corresponds with some of the figures observed by Frobenius in the Fezzan. Somewhat controversially, Frobenius identified this figure with the prototype of the Egyptian god Bes.

Notable among the animals included in these *graffiti* are an ox, composed in the naturalistic style; a lion, viewed face on; an antelope *Aepiceros Melampos* (the equatorial *impala*); and also a singularly beautiful running ostrich and a marching warrior with a long body and finely boned features, armed with a javelin.

It was, however, in the course of Mori's third expedition in 1957-58 that, in the fold of a valley at Tagzelt, he had the good fortune to bring off a discovery marking a decisive stage in Saharan studies. He found a series of large human figures with round heads, drawn frontally, painted on the hollowed mountain face at Ghrub (Tagzelt I), while at Uan Mhuggiag (Tagzelt II) on a rock cornice approximately 16 ft. wide by 1 ft. high, he found a procession of women bearing baskets on their backs. Besides this exodus, as it appears to be, there were pictures of a hippopotamus and a rhinoceros (Plate 1), as well as other pictures evidently of a later date. Finally, in the Uan Amil cave (Tagzelt III) he found the most beautiful of all the Fezzan pictures, works described by such authorities as Biasutti, Cerulli, Graziosi and Grottanelli as being 'of authentic prehistoric genius'.

PLATE A. Initiation ceremony. Rock painting with individual figures of a blond European type. Pastoral period. Tagzelt region of the Acacus Massif, Fezzan, Libya.

The Rock Works

These pictures show a remarkable care in portraiture, which distinguishes them from the generality of rock works, in which the human figure is usually very stylised. This attention to morphological detail, together with the unusual preservation of chromatic values (due perhaps to the use of casein in the original dilution of the colours), has preserved for us the record of a plainly European race. The figures have light skin and fair hair. The hair is arranged characteristically with a lock of hair piled high up on the forehead, reminiscent of the chignon still in use among the Peul or Fulbe women who live in the bends of the Senegal and the Niger. This similarity reinforces the hypothesis that the Peul, who are to-day negroid nomads, may well be of Saharan origin.

The only reference to this sort of hairstyle is made by the Abbé Breuil in his study of the rock pictures of Tassili. He refers to them as the 'yellow caps'; but he is careful to admit the possibility that they were in fact a form of *coiffure*. Mori's discoveries have now enabled us to confirm the Abbé's somewhat tentative hypothesis, for in these rock works are carefully depicted the various stages of preparing these elaborate *coiffures*.

The figures are for the most part elongated. The warriors are armed with bows, the chiefs with boomerangs and a special sort of battle-axe with a hook on the end. The actual scenes represent rites of sexual magic, initiation ceremonies (Plate A), and skirmishes between what appear to be members of the same race, although evidently of different clans. The pictures of animals, especially oxen, are among the best, artistically, of this type of rock work. The composition is skilfully balanced and confers on the animals their special feeling of calm. In design, as in the use of colour, we here witness the height of a mature expression.

In the scene reproduced in Plate A one is immediately struck by the fair hair of the person standing in profile. Nearby, another man, who may or may not be engaged in the same rite, is arranging his hair. The whole scene is permeated with the atmosphere of sacred magic typical of this culture, and recalls the rite of 'the passage under the skin' and the mysterious Tikenu—itself perhaps of Libyan origin—in the initiation ceremonies of Pharaonic Egypt.

Specialists are now studying the various finds made by Mori on his last expedition,* with a view to dating them. Among these are some manufactured bone objects which remind Mori—although he has been careful to avoid jumping to conclusions—of some of the finds in the neolithic village of Merimde in Egypt. There is also a negroid skeleton showing traces of mummification, though this may in fact be due merely to natural dehydration, and to having subsequently been wrapped in the skin of an animal.

Radio-carbon tests of organic matter, together with geological and palaeobotanical study of the rock strata and samples of vegetation, have yielded valuable chronological data. The date of the find has been definitely fixed: the material is clearly contemporary with predynastic Egypt, antedating El Omari. The rock works from which the domestic horse is absent are, however, earlier still. As has already been pointed out, the domestic horse was unknown in the Sahara until 1500 BC, hence such works must precede this date.

The special importance of these wall paintings, apart from their purely aesthetic value, consists in their evidence of the presence in Africa of prehistoric races of a European type—in possession of a definite social order, and endowed with exceptional artistic ability. It is too early yet to draw positive conclusions; but Mori's finds seem to support the belief, already held by many authorities, that there was an influx of Mediterranean races at the time when the North African and Nilotic cultures were beginning to take shape. Mori quotes the opinion of the Abbé Breuil from his work on Tassili, which we have already mentioned: 'Il est à

---

* This was written in 1958. Since then, the results of Mori's IVth Expedition, the one referred to above, have been analysed. See *La Mummia infantile di Uan Muhuggiag*: Fabrizio Mori, e Antonio Ascenzi; *Rivista di Antropologia*, Vol. xlvi, Rome, 1959.

penser que c'est de cet art Bovidien Nord-Africaine que les arts primitifs naturalistes d'Égypte et de Crète sont nés à la fin du Néolithique.' This hypothesis has been accepted, among Egyptologists, by Capart; among art historians by Galassi; and, in the sphere of the spread of Mediterranean influence, by Giulio Del Pelo Pardi, a man deeply cultivated in historical as well as agricultural studies.

In addition to all this, the discovery of the pre-dynastic necropolis of Gabelein by Italian missionaries in Egypt has clearly demonstrated (both from the anthropological evidence, as well as from the type of interment employed) the presence of Mediterranean races on Egyptian soil. It was in fact this discovery that induced Paolo Orsi to ask whether early Sicilians ever penetrated into Egypt; while Mori himself is willing to consider the hypothesis which I myself, on the basis of researches conducted on the spot, have been led to accept: namely, that prehistoric Saharan art influenced the art of Ancient Egypt.

To pass to the Egyptian rock works, H. A. Winkler has outlined the following scheme based on a study of the rock engravings at Wadi Hammamath, between Kena and Assuan in Upper Egypt:

1. *Incisions of early hunters,* either chiselled in a pointillist fashion or incised, and strongly schematic in character. The elephant, crocodile and giraffe are represented, but there are no asses or oxen. These incisions are attributed to the oldest period.

2. *Graffiti of autocthonous mountain dwellers,* generally chiselled. There are a few elephants and a giraffe, while asses and oxen (the latter sometimes with the disk between their horns), appear for the first time. There are also pictures of the domestic horse which then disappears in the first historical period, to reappear with the Hyksos. There are warriors with spears and arrows, beside people worshipping and praying—the first evidence, together with the pictures of sacred animals, of cult forms. According to Winkler these mountain dwellers were of Hamitic

stock. In many of the scenes there are boats of the same type as those reproduced on painted ceramics.

3. *Incisions of foreign invaders*, chiselled and in abstract style. Hunting scenes with the bow and the lasso provide the most frequent subjects. From the fact that the boats are of a different type, appearing to be more seaworthy, Winkler has suggested that these 'invaders' may have come from the east, across the Red Sea. The pictures of this period portray a varied assortment of animals: the elephant, the hippopotamus, the giraffe, the ox, the antelope, the ostrich, the dog, etc.

4. *Incisions of the ancient inhabitants of the Nile Valley*, mostly chiselled and only rarely genuinely incised. The portraits of humans recall those of the autocthonous mountain dwellers, at least in general character. Here again we meet the so-called 'praying figures', or people with upraised arms, while others display Libyan traits. The animals represented are the hippopotamus, the crocodile, the antelope, as well as other animals from earlier periods. The boats are of a river type and would therefore have been used only locally.

The *motifs* of prehistoric Egyptian rock art have survived in the slate palettes of historic times originally used to grind malachite for green eye-shadow which, as well as being a cosmetic, also served as an antiseptic. The practice of engraving these slates was developed in the predynastic period. Here also we find hunting scenes and pictures of local animal life, together with strange figures composed of mythical animals, or of anthropomorphic zoocephalic creatures such as we have seen in the incisions and rock paintings. The original function of these slate palettes was gradually superseded, and they assumed a commemorative and ritual character.

Another field in which historical Egypt inherits the spirit of the rock works is in the enormous carvings on temple walls. Side by side with cult scenes, the emphasis is on the exaltation of the Pharaoh's victories. These scenes are not solely, or even primarily, commemorative: they were intended to maintain the immanent vitality of such forces of supremacy as are symbolised by a sovereign's victory over his enemies. The co-ordinates of this archetypal form remained constant from the earliest historical period of King Narmer's palette, to the close of Pharaonic Egypt.

The roots of predynastic Egypt strike deep into Africa, and it is these roots that have transmitted to later periods a specific mental orientation proper to the 'world of magic'. In Egypt, however, a vital grafting took place. This was due to the rise and development of a superior Mediterranean form of agriculture. In this process the elements of the original substrate achieved their sublimation in a fresh synthesis that is of the very essence of Nilotic culture. The dialogue 'The World and I' was no longer the result of confrontations with forces perennially hostile, but sprang from a partnership in the peaceful reproductive processes of agriculture. In this way the ameliorative characteristics of the world of magic were preserved, and the decline into witchcraft avoided. This decline occurred throughout all other parts of Africa, but not in Egypt for the most, or better, part of its history.

Some of the elements of the substrate culture, however, emerge again in the rites connected with the Pharaoh's coronation. The plait of hair which, as a tail, forms a part of his ceremonial dress and has the effect of integrating the new sovereign with the world of the gods, is connected with the figures of prehistoric Libya (Plate 2). Onomantic magic, and the magic of the image (such as the rite to ward off the dragon Apep, the symbol of evil) belong to the same order of ideas; and such ideas are still found to-day, although in regressive and complex forms, in the ritual practices of many primitive peoples.

On the relationship between Egypt and the rest of Africa the works of Professor Seligman of Oxford are of the first importance. He places such relationships in predynastic times, deriving them from the ancient Hamitic background which Egypt shared with various eastern Negro cultures.

The Libyan rock works have been the object of numerous Italian expeditions, among them those of Pace-Sergi-Caputo, L. Di Caporiacco and Paolo Grazioso. There are also the investigations of Prince Kemal ed-Din, Hassanein Bey, Rholfs, Breuil and Frobenius, and many others; all of these have submitted the rock works to a detailed examination, and have formulated their own theories on their relative dates and their possible sources of derivation. Together with Alimen, and on the basis of the material elaborated by the authorities just mentioned, we can distinguish the following periods:

1. *Hunting period.* This is the oldest epoch. Graziosi connects it with neolithic crafts. Animal life includes elephants, rhinoceri, giraffes, antelope and bulls.
2. *Pastoral period.* This marks a slow transition from the preceding period. Hunting scenes continue to be represented.
3. *Semi-naturalistic work.* The centre for this phase is Gebel Auenat. The human figures wearing head feathers and have tails hanging from their belts.
4. *Recent period,* i.e. in relation to the foregoing. The human figures appear clothed in a tunic shaped like a double triangle. They antedate the age of the camel, whose advent marks the last phase of these works.

On the evidence of the anthropological discoveries of the Pace-Sergi-Caputo expedition, and the bearing these finds have on the penetration of the Garamanti mentioned by Herodotus, Paolo Graziosi is of the opinion that the figures dressed in the double-triangle tunic may be Libyans of Euro-African and not negroid stock.

Among the colours used in the Libyan wall paintings we rarely find either light yellow or white, both of which are commonly found in the Fezzan. On the other hand the works are rich in violet and a beautiful range of reds.

When we come to the equatorial regions we see that the rock works in Abyssinia and in the former Anglo-Egyptian Sudan are clearly related to the pastoral pictures of Gebel

Auenat. There are two main periods, the earlier work being naturalistic, and the latter schematic.

Nigerian work is similarly lacking in original traits. It mostly reflects the style of the Fezzan and lacks the tropical animal life one would expect. However, in the Cameroons the geometric Yagua work, which uses the technique of pointillist chiselling, is of considerable interest, as is that of Katanga and Angola in which the style is schematic. The lines are obtained by means of a succession of small holes. The figures, which are sometimes painted, include groups of humans, animals (among which are snakes, birds and fishes), and schematised aprons for covering the sex parts. These were connected with the pubic ceremonies common to those regions, some of which still survive there. Magic patterns comprised of straight and curved lines, meeting and intersecting, are deeply incised and probably also refer to initiation ceremonies.

In Tanganyika, where the rock works are particularly numerous, seventeen periods have been distinguished, each with its individual style. Those belonging to the earliest period are somewhat crude, but the later work displays a high level of naturalism. This applies to the incisions as well as to the paintings which, judging from the strata in which the colouring materials were found, appear to be among the oldest in Africa.

In a word, whether these works are judged stylistically or from the point of view of the period at which they were composed, one is compelled to agree with Alimen when he speaks of the cultural unity of the equatorial world towards the close of the fourth millennium.

The final stage of our brief survey leads us to South Africa which is the region richest both in paintings and incisions. When the first European observers studied the works in this area, from Rhodesia to the Cape, they did so very superficially, attributing everything indifferently to the Bushmen. To-day, the Bushmen are living in a phase of cultural decline. It is true that they used to, and still do, decorate rock walls with paintings and incisions; but their style and the general quality of their productions are plainly inferior to the older works, which are on the same qualitative level as the bison of Altamira. We are thus faced with cultures different from those of the present day Bushmen. And this is clear not only from the rock works themselves, but also from the related archaeological evidence.

If we move south into southern Rhodesia, a country bounded on the north by the Zambesi and the south by the Limpopo, we are confronted by traces of vast constructions in stone. These are the remains of the civilisation of Zimbabwe, the object of an important expedition by Frobenius. The high walls of the acropolis, the remains of temples, the wide terraces of the Inyanga, the underground stone houses, are the sole evidence of an extremely old kingdom, still flourishing on the arrival of the Portuguese— who lost no time in destroying it.* The wall paintings that abound on the granite hillsides reflect the character of this 'sacred' kingdom.

In the main it is an art of funerary scenes and propitiation ceremonies. Treated as complementary to the surviving oral traditions in the area, it has enabled us to reconstruct the outlines of this ancient kingdom. When we remember that Zimbabwe was an extreme example of a theocracy in which every aspect of life was bound to astronomical events, each of these elements can be seen to have an intrinsic and detailed interest. Unlike Egypt in which the Pharaoh was regarded as the *Ka* of Horus, that is a solar reflex, the Zimbabwe sovereign represented the moon, and his public appearances were strictly regulated to the moon's phases. There was a special cult of the morning star, Venus, who presided over the royal nuptials and strictly controlled sexual relations and the ceremonies attending them. At the end of the year of Venus, a specific astronomical conjunction with the moon marked the end

---

* The Dutch traveller, Dapper, wrote in 1686 that the royal palace was five miles to the west of Sofala, and that the sovereign bore the title *Monomotapa*, or 'Lord of the Mountains', or 'Lord of Work', in reference to the flourishing mining industry (chiefly of gold) in the region.

10. Human mask in bronze. Height 1 ft. 0½ ins. Yoruba.

11. Human mask in bronze. Height 1 ft. Yoruba.

12. Bronze head. The perforations not original.
Life-size. Ife, S. Nigeria.

13. Detail of the head of a king. Bronze. Full height 1 ft. 7 ins. Benin.

14. Girl's head. Bronze. Height 9 ins. Benin.

15. Bronze plaque with two warriors. 1 ft. 7$\frac{1}{2}$ ins. ×1 ft. 1 in.
Benin.

16. Detail of Plate 15.

17. Bronze group of warriors and dignitaries.
1 ft. 2 ins. × 11 ins. Height 11½ ins. Benin.

of the existing reign. The king was violently put to death (ritual regicide) and the sceptre passed to a new sovereign. Aspects of these practices, among others, are reproduced in the wall paintings. Ritual regicide appears in the context of astronomical magic symbolism, together with the reproduction of anthropomorphic and zoocephalic entities. The frontal projection of the human figure is reminiscent of Ancient Egypt, which may be another example of the influence of the African substrate on early Nilotic culture.

These pictures, called by the indigenous inhabitants of the area *madsimu dsangara*, or 'spirits of the forgotten dead', are plainly distinct in style and subject from the productions of the Bushmen. It is, however, difficult to date them with certainty. According to Frobenius this culture, which is connected with the oldest pictures, flourished between the fourth and fifth millennia BC. The frescoes of the Bambata, which are more or less naturalistic in style, have been associated with stone tools of the Wiltonian period which corresponds to the late Palaeolithic in Europe. But the whole question of dating is still open, although it is certain that in the case of the oldest works we have to speak in terms of millennia rather than centuries.

Besides the mythical and ritual scenes found in Rhodesia, there are also, throughout the rock walls of South Africa, elegantly executed animal pictures consisting mostly of elephants, hippopotami, rhinoceri, giraffes, zebras, antelope, baboons and ostriches. The style is naturalistic, but there are also stylised and abstract forms (Plate 3). In addition, one finds mythical creatures such as long-necked monsters with wings, and classical centaurs and 'satyrs' (Plates 4, 5, Drawing 3).

The paintings, particularly of the southern region, are polychrome. Various shades of red were used, obtained from oxide; white obtained from kaolin or from the droppings of birds; and also black. The scenes often have various strata superimposed, which makes identification difficult; for it is not always easy to determine which composition belongs to which strata, or what is their proper chronological order. Some incisions display an extreme subtlety of line, others are chiselled pointillistically; these are without firm contours, or are executed in so fine a manner as to resemble emery paper. M. C. Burkitt and A. J. Goodwin agree with van Riet Lowe in attributing these pictures to the mesolithic period. Frobenius, confining himself mostly to technique, believes that the fact that the incisions have the

Drawing 3. Satyr with female figure. Rock *graffito*. 6 ins. × 11½ ins. Klerksdorp, S. Africa.

same tonality as the rock in which they were cut, sufficiently demonstrates their antiquity, the patina due to weathering having caused the tone of the incision to conform to that of the rock face. As regards style, Frobenius concentrates on the paintings, classifying the differences between the northern style of Rhodesia and that of the Cape region. He describes the northern work as different from the southern in an almost exclusive use of red, with monochrome profiles in which the details have been obtained by means of white dots; the pictures are worked from the periphery, while the successive areas of wall-space are always filled.

The most representative examples of the northern style have been discovered in the Inoro cave, known to have been used from the earliest times until quite recently as a burial vault. In the south, authorities have compared the naturalistic animal pictures to the analogous Franco-Cantabrian works and to those of Eastern Spain. They perceive a stylistic connection from which they deduce a special relationship or derivation; but this subject is outside the limits of our present study. In the Cape Province, three periods have been assigned to the pictures belonging to the epoch before the Bantu invasion. The first period is monochrome. The subjects are isolated and presented in sharp silhouette. The second is bichrome. The pictures are of a wider range, including grouped compositions, and take account of the laws of perspective. The third period is polychrome, and is divided into two: first, 'the gazelles phase', which consists of exquisitely finished compositions; and secondly, the phase of large pictures, which represents the period's artistic peak. The subjects are suffused by an atmosphere of peace and well-being that distinguishes the later works from the earlier. After this there follow the invasions of the Bantu armed with spears and shields. In the pictures of this later phase the Bushmen are depicted trying to defend their beasts from the invaders with bows and arrows. This type of picture would appear to commemorate the turbulence that broke the preceding calm. The figures are represented dynamically and with a certain descriptive power. There are also mythical scenes on the subject of death, and there are numerous pictures of creatures with animal heads. These so greatly overshadow the other figures that, instead of calling them masked men, it would be truer to describe them as beings of the suprasensible world, dramatically visualised by this specific ethnic psyche.

We have already mentioned that the existence of such entities, often considered harmful, is a veritable fact among various African peoples; and that by means of the metamorphic powers of witchcraft they are often associated with certain animal species, in which forms they assume a totem aspect. This is shown in the Cameroons, where the members of secret societies acknowledge a bond with specific animals such as the leopard, the serpent, the hyena, etc., rather than with the totem of the clan or tribe. This bond is called 'union' (*Ket*). It presupposes a complex ritual of which the prime purpose is to induce a state of ecstasy. When such a state is attained, psychic fusion takes place with the occult forces of whatever animal pertains to the rite, and this will in some way correspond to a specific mark borne by the individual. Among the Bandjuns of the Cameroons, union with the chimpanzee is called *Ket-pu-kop* and is found in opposition to union with the leopard, *Ket-num-goi*. Men-leopards are found in the Yabassi region where, clothed in leopard skins, and armed with iron harpoons with five points, like a leopard's claws, they kill the human victims who have been allotted to them.

3

AFRICAN CIVILISATIONS

The rock works that we have been examining are like so
many rays of light refracted from the facets of the black
diamond. They provide isolated and brilliant illumination,
but of themselves they do not yield the detailed information
we are looking for concerning the oldest African cultures.
For that we have to rely on archaeological research. This is
the case with the 'civilisation of Nok' which quite recent
discoveries have brought to light. As African archaeological
researches are still in progress and have been confined solely
to limited areas, we lack the facts necessary to draw even
preliminary conclusions, or to establish the necessary
correlations between the cultures of later periods. Besides
this, the corruptibility of many of the materials used means
that valuable evidence is lost and makes one very cautious
about dating. In a later chapter we shall have occasion to
look at the survivals of these lost cultures, some of them as
old as the first millennium BC.

For more recent periods, we fortunately have a wealth
of material left us by travellers and chroniclers. Besides
the first Greek records of Herodotus, there are the reports
of Roman generals, the fabulous descriptions of Mohammedan historians, and finally the stories of European
navigators and explorers. There is a mass of material from
the sixth century AD to to-day. It is heterogeneous and
lacking in objectivity, because of the feelings of passion
and partisanship that frequently inspired the compilation.
Nevertheless, it is an invaluable source of information. By
internal comparison, and comparison with the archaeological and enthnographic evidence, we can, with some
certitude, reconstruct the histories of the various African
empires.

Introduction to African Art

We shall, however, trace the barest outline of these histories, only touching briefly on some of their outstanding features. The sole purpose of what follows is to provide the reader with a framework in which, finally, to examine the picture. Were this study to be an examination merely of the ethnographic manifestations of the various tribes, it would be a different matter. But to begin with we undertook to present only the *best* example of African 'art' and, if this is to be done, it is necessary to give due weight to the socio-historical substrate in which the product has its roots. A rich court that is inclined to patronage will require from its artists products for purposes of display and decoration quite distinct from the functional objects that are strictly limited to ritual and magical use. This is the case with, among other examples, Yoruba statuary and the Benin bronzes. The connection between the two sorts of 'artistic' production is solely ethnic.

Finally, North Africa and Egypt are necessarily excluded from our survey. Although displaying the clearest psycho-morphological links with the Black Continent, they fall outside the scope of our present study. Nevertheless, as occasion demands, we shall draw attention to the elements those civilisations have in common with the African substrate.

West Africa is our point of departure: a region which appears to have been the seat of the most powerful kingdoms. The first, in order of time, is the kingdom of Ghana, founded in the year AD 300. The people, known as the Fula, were of mixed race and obscure origin, and lived under a matriarchy. The country was so rich in gold that, as we know, the region came, in later times, to be called 'The Gold Coast'. On the basis of exporting gold dust, trade rapidly developed, bringing riches and well-being to the people. The capital town, Ghana, gave its name to the kingdom, which in due course transformed itself into an Empire stretching from the Atlantic to Timbuktu in the east, and to Bamako in the south. Towards the end of the eighth century the throne was occupied by sovereigns of Soninké stock. They lived in surroundings of great

34

magnificence, with crystal windows and frescoes on their walls.

Scenes worthy of the *Arabian Nights* have been preserved by Arab historians such as Ibn Khaldun and El-Idrisi and in the chronicles *Tarikh-el Fettach* and *Tarikh-es-Sudan*. The reader is bewildered by descriptions of a blend of ostentation and refinement that seem downright baroque. The effect is far indeed from the stereotyped picture of naked savages dancing round a totem pole. One reads of solid stone houses, clothes of silk and velvet, and armour studded with ivory and silver. Every evening, seated on a carved golden throne, the sovereign attended a banquet at which he offered choice food and rare wines to 10,000 of his subjects. We are told that Caligula liked to bring his horse to table: Kanissai, King of Ghana, not to be outdone, ordained that his 10,000 horses should sleep only on precious rugs, and that they should be fettered with pure silk. And not only that, but he instructed three persons to be permanently attached to the chariot of each horse, with suitably shaped bronze vessels in which they might catch the sacred urine. The entire milieu is one in which a golden luxury seems to have run riot: opulence is everywhere.

However, a culture founded on impermanent values rather than on radical ones such as are derived from agriculture, cannot last long. Cupidity in the shape of lustful neighbours will soon break loose; and in fact Ibn Khaldun tells us that 50,000 of them, mounted on Mehari camels and constituting the following of the Berber King of Lemtuna, laid waste the entire region of Augam. This was only the first of many onslaughts against the Imperial power, which were destined to increase steadily in severity. Thus in AD 1020 the Berbers renewed their attacks. They left a wake of devastation behind them, extending the length of their long march; but, above all, they laid the foundation of a dangerous alliance with a fanatical sect of Mohammedans, the Almoravidi. In its present form the word is a Spanish corruption of the original term *El-Morabethin*, or 'People of *Ribat*', that is, 'of the monastery'.

Under the specious pretext of a 'holy war' against the infidels who refused to accept the faith of Islam, the Almoravidi, together with the Berbers, made repeated attacks on Ghana and, of course, her riches. In the year 1054, the city of Audaghost, a dependency of Ghana, was occupied and its inhabitants massacred.

In order to confront the growing menace Ghana raised an army of 200,000 men, of whom 40,000 were bowmen. With these she succeeded, in 1060, in containing the forces of the Emperor of Morocco, an Almoravidi ally of the Berbers. But the end was not far off. In 1076, Abu Bekr ben Omar, again under the pretext of a 'holy war', moved against Ghana and delivered the death blow. All resistance was extinguished. There followed a period of protracted spoliations and plunder. This aftermath was so severe, that it set in motion migratory movements of entire populations —for example, that of the Akan group towards the south. In 1087, Abu Bekr was killed, and this allowed the Soninké to retrieve, at least temporarily, something of their former power. They pieced together the fragments of Ghana's shattered Empire, managing to keep it in being for a little more than a century longer. At length, in the year 1203, Sumanguru, Emperor of the Sosso, once vassals of Ghana, placed the city and the entire region under his sovereignty.

In the meantime, to the east, another imperial power, that of Songhai, was on the rise. The first dynasty had been founded in the year AD 690, and in the veins of the ruling race, the Dia or Za, there ran both Berber and Negro blood. According to El-Bekri, the Songhai king was converted to Islam in 1010; but he left his people free to profess the faith of their forefathers, that is, ancestor worship. It is therefore clear that the King's decision to embrace Islam was an able political move, designed to consolidate powerful alliances, rather than a true conversion. Gao, the capital of the Empire, was a flourishing trading centre whose most active period coincided with temporary subjection to the Empire of Mali which occurred in 1325.

According to El-Idrisi, Gao's markets were rich in gold,

rice and fish, and contracts for these goods were drawn up with distant countries. As with Ghana, the culture was founded on commerce: to use a term of economic science, it was a mercantile culture. Precisely because of this, new needs bred new demands, and the periods of greatest activity were characterised by a feverish rhythm. Caravans, the sign of an active export and import trade, were continually setting out and arriving from far-distant parts. In 1335, a Songhai prince, Ali Kolen, who had been held as a hostage at the Mali court, returned to Gao where he assumed the title of *Sonni*, or 'liberator'. This was the beginning of the Sonni dynasty of Songhai, which numbered nineteen sovereigns and lasted from 1335 to 1493.

Notable among the rulers of this dynasty was Sonni Ali, who came to the throne in 1474. He led his country in war and planned her prosperity in peace. Having reconquered Timbuktu and Gienne he devoted his energies to peaceful works. In particular he promoted the benefits that spring from agriculture by establishing a network of hydraulic canals throughout the country. His reign was characterised by a violent reaction against Mohammedans, from which, however, men of learning were exempted. 'Without them,' said Sonni Ali, 'the world would lack grace and pleasure.'

Soninké Mohammed Turé, Sonni Ali's successor, was similarly inclined. He was a Soninké of Negro extraction and founded the new dynasty of the Askias. He surrounded himself with learned men, and transformed Timbuktu, Gao, Walata and Gienne into important centres of learning whose fame spread even beyond the limits of Africa. The University of Timbuktu attracted Arab law students by promoting such historical research as that which produced the chronicles known as *Tarikh-el-Fettach* and *Tarikh-es-Sudan* which have been mentioned above. The name 'Askia' appears to have referred to the cry with which the daughters of Sonni Ali greeted the news that Mohammed Turé, formerly one of their father's lieutenants, had seized the throne: *A si kyi a!* i.e., 'That he will never be!' Taking up the challenge, Mohammed proclaimed that from that moment the death cry of the Sonni dynasty would be the motto of the new.

Askia Mohammed I was a ruler who combined legislative ability with high military qualities. In preference to the previous practice of raising troops as they were needed, he laid the foundations of a regular army. He instituted a rigid court protocol with a court chamberlain, and reorganised the system of imposts and the administration of cults. He arranged that, side by side with Mohammedan institutions, the rites of ancestor worship should be allowed to continue under the supervision of an animistic high priest.

After Mohammed's deposition in 1528, Gao for some time maintained the position it had reached under his rule. The picture of Gao left us by Leo Africanus is one of lordly palaces and abundant goods evenly distributed among the various classes of the community, such as farmers, fishermen and merchants. It is recorded that Askia Mohammed's sons wrested the throne from their old father and exiled him, first on an island and then in Gao, where the great king died in 1542. Half a century later, Gao, and with it the Songhai Empire, was forced to capitulate to the Moroccan forces of Giuba Pasha, who were equipped with the first firearms.

Solid as a rock in the middle of the rising tide of Islam, the Empire of Mosi remained faithful to its traditional institutions, notably the cult of ancestor worship, disdaining any form of compromise with the new faiths. Situated between the Songhai Empire and the southern forests, it was, until the eleventh century, a species of confederation between the kingdoms of Wagadugu, of Yatenga and of Gurmantché. The first of these constituted the Empire of Mosi, properly so called. It had a firm constitutional structure based on provincial divisions and vassal kingdoms. In their turn these were subdivided into districts and villages. A system of checks and balances between the various state organs prevented the abuse of power. The king was chosen by an indirect elective system. A council of elders selected the candidates for the throne from among the heads of the most important families. In addition, as a safeguard against the rise of despotism, the king was assisted in his functions by the animistic high priest, the regional governors, and the council of elders.

A strict court protocol was in force in this empire also. Audience with the king, known as *Morho-Nabba*, was held in the morning in the seat of the council of state, and in the evening in the court of justice. The economy was evenly balanced between agriculture and mercantilism. Although on a smaller scale, the Kingdom of Yatenga, bordering Gao and Mali, and that of Gurmantché, shared the same constitutional basis as the Mosi Empire. The stability of the institutions of these kingdoms and the spiritual cohesion existing among their peoples kept them, until recent times, free from the corrosive effect of foreign influence.

But to recapture the fabulous atmosphere of the *Arabian Nights* we must turn to the Empire of Mali, known also as Mandé, Mandingo, or Malinké. In 1203, when the Sosso king, Sumanguru, was leading a campaign against Ghana, he discovered that the kingdom of Mali, till then insignificant, was fast becoming a major power. Following one of the first rules of war, 'attack before being attacked', Sumanguru sprang the first blow by eliminating all the heirs to the throne of Mali. Only one son, Sundiata, was left alive; and he was a cripple. In the course of time, grown to manhood, and cured of his infirmity, Sundiata—also known as Mari Jata—succeeded to the throne of his forefathers. In 1235 he met and slew Sumanguru and united the Empire of Mali and the Kingdom of Sosso under one crown. It is traditionally asserted that in 1240 Sundiata razed Shana itself to the ground, but the episode is obscure. In the writings of Raimond Lullo, we read that a Pontifical envoy visited the city in the fourteenth century and reported that its government was pledged to 'idolatrous princes who worship the sun, the stars, the birds and the beasts, and that the Negroes were very tall and lived without any law'.

Sundiata made himself master of the gold mines of Bambuk, by extending the boundaries of the Empire as far as the regions of the Wolof. His name was venerated for centuries, and his warlike exploits became the subject of legend and popular poetry. On his death in 1285, the throne was usurped by a freed-man, Sakura, who raised the economic level of the country by skilful trade agreements. On his return from a pilgrimage to Mecca, however, Sakura was assassinated and the kingdom sank back into the penumbra of mediocre powers until 1307, when Kankan Mussa ascended the throne.

Kankan Mussa, also known as *Mansa* or 'sultan', was similarly destined to enter the world of legend. He was determined that the world should recognise the splendour of his kingdom. When, therefore, he made his pilgrimage to Mecca in 1324, he travelled with a caravan of 60,000 men, who constituted the royal retinue. According to El Mamer, 12,000 of these were clothed in brocaded silk, while 500 preceded the sovereign, each bearing a bar of gold weighing more than $5\frac{1}{2}$ lb. The caravan was followed by eighty camels, each loaded with 264 lb. of gold. El Mamer remarks that the appearance of so much gold produced a notable devaluation in that commodity throughout the Middle East.

When he returned from Mecca, Kankan Mussa brought with him the famous poet Es-Saheli, a native of Granada, where he had also acquired fame as an architect. He was commissioned to design a mosque in Gao, and various palaces in Timbuktu. The patronage of the throne stimulated the growth of cultural centres, such as the University of Sankore, where celebrated philosophers and jurists established themselves. The historian, Ibn Batuta, records that ideas of law and justice were particularly developed among the Mali.

We know little of the period following the eclipse of Kankan Mussa in 1332. But Mali continued to exercise her suzerainty over vast areas for a long time. In 1455, the Venetian navigator, Cadamosto, referred to her domination in the region of Gambia. Later, the Empire of Mali was succeeded by that of Songhai, and the centre of economic life shifted to Gao.

In 1591 the Songhai Empire collapsed, and bands of Moroccans occupied Timbuktu and Gao. There followed a long period in which armed marauders plundered and devastated the neighbouring regions. From the beginning of their penetration into the Black Continent, when they initiated the slave-trade, the Arabs had been restlessly pushing forward in a ceaseless search for new areas of exploitation. Among others, the Lake Chad district, the Eastern Sudan and Zanzibar were the objects of frequent incursions; and through the centuries regular caravan routes provided Morocco, Egypt and Arabia with a continual flow of slaves. The Portuguese slave-trade developed along the coastal regions towards the middle of the fifteenth century, increasing in intensity as rivalry grew between the European slave dealers. The region where the traffic was briskest became known on the maps as 'The Slave Coast'. Under such conditions it was almost impossible for a people like the Massina or Bambara to keep their independence, or to remain—even for a short time—in a state of social consolidation.

The Massina Kingdom lasted from the seventeenth to the nineteenth century. Its fall was hastened by the conversion of King Seku Hamed (1810-44) to Islam, an event which encouraged the Fula population to do likewise. When they were converted they became, as so often happens, fanatical persecutors of those who had remained loyal to their traditional cults. The Bambara (Banmana) Empire arose in the seventeenth century. It occupied the Segu region, and was the result of the local population freeing themselves from Mali rule. They experienced a period of prosperity based on a flourishing agriculture before being completely destroyed by the Massina troops of El Hagi Omar in 1854. Although a religious motive was again found for the massacre and subsequent plunder (for Bambara had remained unrepentantly pagan to the end), we have only to observe the meaning of the word 'Bambara' in Arabic (slave flesh) to be aware of the true nature of the Mohammedan occupation.

In remote epochs various kingdoms arose along the coast who managed to maintain their independence for a long time. Tekrur, in Senegal, mentioned by the historian Idrisi, was one of these. There were also the Wolof, Sine and Baol kingdoms in the district of Serere, the theocratic state of Futa and, in the forest regions, the Kingdom of Baule. Here, and in the neighbouring Ashanti kingdoms whose products were used in cult practices, goldsmith work reached a fine pitch of development. The bronze weights used to measure gold were also beautifully worked. And to these we shall return later. The Ashanti Kingdom was at its height between 1700 and 1895 when it had to bow before British occupation. In 1700, Osai Tutu, who was one of the greatest Ashanti kings, inaugurated the use of a wooden throne which was affirmed to be of divine origin.

The Kingdom of Dahomey had from the beginning a complex socio-political organisation together with a powerful standing army. Leo Africanus mentions its existence in 1507, but its foundation has not yet been firmly established. The fourth king, King Agasa, formed a squadron of a thousand Amazons, each vowed to chastity. They were intended to complete the army, and their exploits became legendary in Europe. The military character of this kingdom is symbolised by a unique piece of African statuary (Plate 30): a bronze effigy of the god of war, part of the treasure of King Behanzin, the last king of Dahomey who, in 1904, offered strong resistance to the French occupation.

In early times, the Kingdom of Yoruba attained a high artistic level. The terracottas and bronzes of Ife are classic pieces of African art, so much so that Frobenius suggested that the area might well have been the site of the mythical Atlantis. The artistic school of Ife exercised a considerable influence on Benin, the neighbouring kingdom. Ife during the early centuries probably produced works in bronze.

Little is known of the origins of Benin. Their kings (*Oba*) claimed to be of divine origin, and in their myths on this subject it may be possible to trace a connection with the Ife culture, in whose pantheon is the god Olokun, who is fabled as having brought their civilisation from the sea. About the year 1270 under the rule of Oba Oguola, the city of Benin was fortified and surrounded by a wall. The Portuguese established trading relations with it in the fifteenth century, and in 1686 the Dutch navigator, Dapper, described the city in enthusiastic terms. He mentions no less than thirty main streets. The artisans' quarters, he says, were laid out in sections according to their craft. The royal palace was 'larger than the city of Haarlam, with splendid galleries as large as the Bourse at Amsterdam'. The wooden pillars of these galleries were decorated with bronze plaques, one of the more characteristic features of Benin art. Between the visits of Dapper and another Dutch navigator, Nyandael, in 1704, the city was destroyed, and the plaques disappeared from the pillars. The city itself, however, recovered and was gradually rebuilt.

The *coup de grâce* to the Benin civilisation was delivered by British troops in the course of a 'punitive expedition' in the year 1897. The year before a party of 250 British soldiers, ignoring the Oba's warning, had penetrated the city while a religious ceremony was taking place. The party was considered to have profaned the rites which it had interrupted, and was massacred. This gave the British Governor the excuse to organise a 'punitive expedition'. The city was looted and burnt. Three thousand bronze pieces were plundered, which now adorn our European museums and various private collections. Thus ended an artistic tradition exercised uninterruptedly on African soil for at least a thousand years and perhaps longer. Not the least cause of the decline of Benin was the remorseless operation of the slave-trade. In 1852, one vessel alone carried more than 1,200 slaves to the Cuban market. The kingdoms of Sikaso, Liptako, Senufo and Kong all flourished in the hinterland. They were small but industrious centres of artistic activity, noted for their copper and iron work. In the sixteenth century, Hausa was particularly well known for its cotton and hides, although writers such as Leo Africanus mention it as existing even earlier. Agriculture was widely practised especially at Katsina. Other states in the East such as Bornu, Kanem, and Baghirmi, were of limited importance. Arab influence was particularly strong in Wadai, Dar-Fur and Kordofan.

The Loango Kingdom and the Empire of the Congo were both situated between the Gulf of Guinea and the river Congo. They are mentioned by the Portuguese as early as the fourteenth century. The states comprising the Kingdom of Ansika included the Bateke and Bayaka peoples. They were famous for their artistic productions, as were the people of the Kingdom of Bakuka (or Bushongo), one of the more important stylistic centres. We have dealt with the Kikuyu and some of their institutions in an earlier chapter. Later in the book we shall look at the productions of the Babuba, the Warega (or Balega), and of various other tribes.

The object of the historical outline given above has been to draw attention to the existence, in Africa of past days, of autonomous national institutions and powers that constituted the matrix of the formal and stylistic variations met with in African art.

18. Warrior. Detail of Plate 17. Height 1 ft.

19. Bronze panther. 2 ft. 5½ ins. × 1 ft. 5½ ins. Benin.

20. Leopard on bronze plaque. Length 1 ft. 8 ins. Benin.

21. Bronze cock. 1 ft. $7\frac{1}{2}$ ins. × 1 ft. 7 ins. Benin.

22. Bronze plaque with two panthers' heads. 16th-17th centuries. Length 5 ft. 10 ins. Benin.

23. Detail of carved elephant tusk. Full height
about 5 ft. 2 ins.

24. Leopard in ivory. Length 1 ft. 7 ins. Benin.

25. Human mask in ivory. Height 10 ins. Benin.

26. Ivory cup. Height 6 ins. Benin.

4

THE CREATIVE PROCESS

We have already indicated the unsatisfactory nature of the word 'art' in the phrase 'African Art' where an aesthetic analysis based on the Kantian definition of beauty is inapplicable. If the phrase is to be used at all it must be recognised as a purely conventional one. I made the same point in my book *Egyptian Art*, by drawing attention to its magico-religious and, particularly, eschatological character. Sculpture, bas-reliefs, pictures, all serve a specific end, their creation being based on rules belonging to the world of magic. There are thus close points of contact between Egyptian artistic conceptions and those proper to Black Africa. Above all, they both lack a word for 'the Beautiful'.

In ancient Egyptian, as in most African languages, the word for 'beauty' means 'good' or 'harmonious', or 'that from which nothing is lacking'—a definition that reminds one of Constantine Brancusi's aphorism: 'Le beau c'est l'equité absolue.' Such ideas were partly covered in Egypt by the term '*nefer*' (or '*nofre*'). One of the titles of Osiris, '*Unnofré*', usually translated as 'the Good Being', is now thought, according to the most recent studies, to comprise the idea of 'Complete Being'. We are thus led to the roots of a common heritage of thought in which the Beautiful is perceived in the realisation of a state of harmony: not an end in itself, but capable of an integrative function.

In Egypt, integration releases the individual *ego* from the laws of cyclical change. In Africa, integration effects communion with the clan, and participation on a hyperphysical plane, in the drama of creation. The purpose of the highest African initiation rituals is to experience the forces that preside over every tangible manifestation and,

in so doing, achieve a state of psychic fusion with the
generative processes. The precise means of doing this will
vary from tribe to tribe; but analogous objects such as
masks, statues and ritual instruments, are used everywhere.

We have already drawn attention to the metamorphic
power of the mask in pubic initiation ceremonies in which
the adolescent is integrated into the life of the tribe. The
function of the mask is not symbolic but substantial. It
directly influences the psyche by association with the
suffering entailed in the circumcision rites. The mask is
used in the same way in ancient Egypt where it forms part
of the initiation rites of the neo-circumcised who have also
undergone hard physical tests and been subdivided into
age groups. Evidence of this is provided by the Naga
ed-Deir stele, now in Chicago, and by a bas-relief of the
Old Empire which is to be found in the British Museum
and has been interpreted by Stracmans. Again, when the
funeral priest performs his ritual practices on the mummy
of the deceased, it is the jackal mask that renders these
practices efficacious, whereby the original relation between
the god Anubis and his father Osiris is re-established. The
mimed re-enacting of Anubis mummifying Osiris plays its
part, but it is the mask which induces a state of consciousness capable of transporting the participator to the
actual psychic level on which the mythical event took place.

Keeping in mind what has already been said, it is plain
that our normal aesthetic valuations are inadequate in a
context such as this. To describe a mask as 'beautiful' or
'ugly' is merely to express an individual subjective opinion.
In relation to African 'art' such an opinion is, strictly,
pointless. What we must ask ourselves is: 'Can this object
fulfil the purpose for which it was made?' Here we have a
species of functionalism, the search for an adequate
relation between an object and its end, between potency
and act, or between the tangible reality and the transcendent manifestation which it serves. This is the essence
of African so-called 'artistic' work.

The object is the bearer of the vital force, *nyama*. Its form establishes the spatial confines of this force as well as its 'radiating capacity', that is to say, its ability to radiate outwards beyond itself. This presupposes not only the existence of such vital forces, and the possibility of concentrating them in specific objects, but also the participation of someone who is able to make contact with them by the proper use of these objects. This person is of course the sculptor, considered as magician or witch; and his work consists of a series of ritual acts, from the actual assembly of the basic materials to the consecration of the object. These acts are often performed in a peculiar emotional state, 'a sacred fire' artificially induced by means of magic.

The plastic forms of the objects themselves are partly dictated by tribal convention, but are essentially the result of what the psyche has 'seen' in specific states of ecstasy. The Pahuin call these states *ngwel*, while among the Ubanghi-Shari the initiate is known as *so a-gwe tâ na du ti hinga*, 'he who has truly penetrated into the depths of consciousness'. Introspection such as this permits what has been 'seen' in the 'descent to the Underworld' to be objectified in dramatic terms. It canalises the latent forces of the human organism while ensuring that contact is re-established with the causal plane. In this case, the style of a specific object, a mask for example, is simply the record of a particular tribe's vision of suprasensible reality, and is subject to all the variations of similar visions in the temporal order.

The artist 'sees', though in a more fully integrated fashion, with the eyes of the group to which he belongs: his vision is the vision of the clan. This is the explanation of the morphological origins of these productions. As for the so-called 'rites of animation', these recall similar practices used in ancient Egypt. The priest, known as *Sem*, went into a trance corresponding to the Pahuin *ngwel*. In the state of trance he established a connection between the statue of the dead person and his *Ka*, or double. This sort of Egyptian statuary was the product of a sacred art which, in the case of statues of the gods, was attended by complex consecration rites.

In Egypt, the co-ordinates of a geometric 'canon' held to be the expression of celestial laws of harmony, crystallised in set forms, and these determined a style to which her artists remained faithful for thousands of years. This style was directly influenced by a solar theology and by the notion of the resurrected Osiris. The canon of the just proportion reflects the law of Maat, the goddess of abstract Truth and Justice—two terms that were equivalent in ancient Egypt. The Egyptian theocracy was solar-oriented, the Pharaoh himself being a terrestrial reflection of the sun god Horus.

In African cultures, on the other hand, this crystallisation of styles does not occur. The experiences of the individual *ego* find a substitute in collective, that is, tribal integration. Solar magic is replaced by lunar witchcraft, and the importance of the moon in various African ceremonies has been the subject of numerous studies. One is reminded of the civilisation of Zimbabwe in which the king was regarded as a lunar reflex, and whose public appearances were regulated according to the moon's phases, his reign terminating in an act of ritual regicide, occasioned by a specific lunar conjunction.

It is at the full moon that ritual dances are performed and the more violent tribal rites take place. Sexual ceremonies are particularly likely to be conditioned by the moon. The state of ecstasy induced by the masked dances is attributed to lunar influence, as being the plane on which ghosts and spirits have their being. The Baluba used to exhibit their statues to the light of the new moon in order to relate the image to the psychic level on which the moon was believed to operate.

It is true that we find examples of invocations, hymns and praises to the sun, especially in its generative aspect; but the psychic characteristic of all Black African civilisations is lunar and not solar; and this is reflected in the artistic productions of the various tribes, at once determining their sphere of efficacy, and investing them with a characteristic appearance directly related to their essential conception. In the creation of its products, as in all its other manifestations, an African culture is perfectly self-consistent and logical. Lévi-Bruhl's theories on the 'pre-logical' mentality of so-called 'primitive' peoples have had their day. According to him, such people were so ignorant that they did not even understand the laws of nature. They had not yet reached the stage of distinguishing between cause and effect, or identities and contradictions. Although Lévi-Bruhl's theories may seem strange to us, they achieved a certain acceptance at the time, and are probably due to the fact that he was unable himself to engage in field work, but had to be satisfied with second and third hand material. In particular he relied on the reports of missionaries, whose mental training and orientation least qualifies them to understand the nature of the facts that they record.

In place of the 'pre-logical' state, William Fagg posits a 'pre-philosophical' one. He does so with due reservations, however, since he not only admits the logicality of an African's mental processes, but also the existence of an African philosophy. And indeed the theology, cosmology and eschatology of each of the various tribes are not in the least inconsistent within themselves, while the conceptual and dogmatic differences between the tribes are probably less striking than the wide and complex range of theological systems elaborated by the ecclesiastical schools of Pharaonic Egypt. The idea of a God-Creator, anthropomorphic and indifferent to his own creation (which in its turn is indifferent to him), is common to all tribes. It is, as we have seen, only in the most exceptional circumstances that any attempt is made to establish contact with him. Between this Absolute Being and the world there are various planes of being on which exist 'the roots of things': those forces that mould the shapes of the phenomenal world, that animate nature and, in so doing, become personalised. The Creative Being is thought of as hermaphroditic, a trait it passes on to human individuals whose proper sex is confirmed only by initiation rites. The bi-frontal 'Janus masks' (one face male, the other female), are an example of this concept. They are used when the sex of the god addressed is unknown, just as Latin farmers, in the very early days of Rome, used when in doubt to begin a prayer with the invocation, '*Sive deus, sive dea*'.

Gods, ghosts, spirits are always at hand, and men resort to them rather than to the Supreme Being. Above all, recourse is had to ancestral spirits, with whom it is considered essential to establish bonds of communion. Ancestor worship is in fact at the heart of African religion. The shades of the dead, moreover, can return to importune the living, and suitable protection is required against such revenants. This is the function of a funerary image. It attracts to itself the spirit of the deceased so that it becomes locked in the image, thus averting an unfavourable intervention in human affairs. A corresponding belief is found in ancient Egypt, together with the practice of supplying the spirit of the dead person with food offerings which it is supposed to absorb.

Perhaps it might be as well at this point to define what an African thinks are the constituent elements of an individual, and what happens to these elements after death. The physical body is provided with tangible individual support. It is in continuous union with a counterpart, a sort of shadow or 'double', like the Egyptian *Ka*. This double can in special circumstances withdraw itself and become manifest on the plane that the Pahuin call *ngwel*. In the Cameroons the Sara call this double *Koi*. There is also the higher soul, which they call *giekodi*. The Ekoi declare: 'When a man's body decomposes, a new image is formed from it, in every respect like the man when he was alive.' And the Wasu say: 'What is separated from the body after death is the shadow.' This shadow is called *Itongo* by the Zulu, while the Bini refer to it according to circumstances either as 'traveller' or 'guide'. Thus the essential elements comprising an individual are his physical body, his double and his soul. To these must be added the vital breath, which is the dynamic force animating every living creature, which has the power of reincarnating itself in some new form at the moment of death. Finally, there is the name. This sets the seal on a person's individuality while reinforcing the all-important ancestral bonds.

The name is the essence of the thing named. (As witness the demiurgic creation by means of the Word.) It is therefore logical that if an individual is comprised of a number of elements he should also be possessed of a number of names. Thus a man has three names. The first is given him at birth: it cannot change and refers to his individual essence. The second, acquired at his initiation, confirms his new individuality as a full member of the tribe. The third is connected with his physical body, and is the name by which he is usually called. The first two names are secret, for they contain the individual's personality; and an enemy who knew them would, by employing onomantic magic, obviously be in a position to harm him. Exactly the same conception is met with in Egypt. It is therefore fitting that, because of the magic power of the name, the artistic productions of both Egypt and Black Africa should be anonymous. The artist is a craftsman, more or less talented, an interpreter capable of translating into plastic or pictorial terms the elements of his psychic perception. But he is not therefore a 'creator'. Only if he *were* a creator would he have the right to link his name with his 'creation'. This is why practically all Egyptian art is anonymous. The very rare exceptions belong to special moments in history, such as the artistic productions at Tell el Amarna which were the result of the patronage of the Pharaoh Akhenaton. But these only prove the rule.

When a person dies, the elements of which he has been composed are dispersed. The body returns to the earth with which it mingles. The 'double' is able to manifest itself again for a given period and, in so doing, to disturb the peace of those left behind; but it also is ultimately destined for a dissolution as complete as that of the physical body. The soul remains in contact with its descendants. It will continue to exercise an influence for good or ill on tribal fortunes according to the tribe's conduct. Lastly, the vital breath is reassumed into the cosmic economy by animating a new living being.

There is plainly nothing illogical or 'pre-logical' here. Although the Sudanese Bantu exemplify these conceptions particularly clearly, they are common to all African cultures. The vision has of course a specific ethnic character, but it is perfectly consistent in its relationship of cause and effect. Each natural fact has its explanation, even if it is not a scientific one, and this explanation is 'seen', or experienced, in the individual's active participation in phenomenal development.

African thought hinges on the idea of fertility in its many forms, the principle notion being that all organic life on earth, including humanity, has its place in the cosmic economy. It is thus necessary to exalt the vital energy, *nyama*, on which the cosmos is nourished, in all the forms and shapes in which it is found. In its plastic-dynamic form this idea moulds social institutions, rites, individual lives and artistic productions. With this in mind, one should not be surprised that, in sculpting human figures, particular emphasis should be placed on the genital organs.

The erotic dances, performed collectively, and the rites of field and furrow, all have one aim: that of liberating specific forces capable of harmonising with the processes of nature. Fecundity attracts fecundity, and a pregnant woman is therefore placed before the seed at the time of sowing. Thus the cult of nature's personified forces, invariably has as its object a good harvest.

It is in this framework, in the context of this *forma mentis*, that the African artist finds his *raison d'être*. He becomes a maker of technical instruments each of which has its own well-defined use. A statue of an ancestor, a mask, a carved staff used in one of the dances, or an amulet, all are strictly functional. Aesthetic valuation—and this cannot be emphasised too strongly—is totally out of place in relation to such work.

Sculpture of this sort makes good the deficiencies of

human nature by acting as a sort of compensatory or counterbalancing factor. Is somebody ill? The witch-doctor is ready to sculpt an image. He consecrates it by charging it with *nyama*. In order to establish a *rapport* between it and the sick person, he places some particles of organic matter in the image, such as the patient's nails, blood or hair. He then 'strikes' the sickness by driving a nail into that part of the image which corresponds to the relevant ailment. The same procedure is applied if one wishes to harm a distant enemy. Any ethnographic museum possesses at least one of these curious wooden images studded with iron nails, and looking very much like a hedgehog. This is the field of witchcraft as practised in Egypt itself, and as it has survived in modern times among various civilised communities. The context in which such objects are produced, and the essential motives which dictated their forms, are obviously essential to any judgement we may wish to make. To judge them in and for themselves is to indulge in a purely subjective evaluation.

From what has been said it will be plain that such an art will exist only as long as the faith which gave it birth. When that particular vision of the world collapses (and there will be many reasons for such a collapse, notably colonialism and the introduction of new faiths), it will become increasingly difficult to infuse life into the corresponding 'art' forms.

A genuine link with the old traditions and with the spiritual vision proper to Black Africa survives to-day in only the most limited areas. Elsewhere, the collapse of the old ideas together with the imposition of an utterly foreign sensibility, with new ethical conceptions, has determined the rise of aberrant art forms. These are westernised or industrialised, produced with an eye solely to tourist exploitation. There is, fortunately, a reaction against such forms, which indicates the direction in which African art may possibly develop in the future. We shall examine these reactions in the last chapter.

To return to the works of the past, another important

feature must be mentioned. That is, the predominance of the sacred over the profane. This applies equally whether the works are considered from the point of view of chronology or from that of subject-matter. It is a predominance that directly influenced the minor and decorative arts. The type of instrument in daily use, a man's clothes and *coiffure*, were invested with a sacramental value; and this was due to an inherently religious orientation only to be expected under a theocratic form of government. The decorative *motifs* in ornamental work, in jewellery, in engravings and in the symbolism of the clan, all express the same recurrent preoccupation with sexuality and the need to promote fertility. The universe, the world, the tribe, the family and the couple, provide endless subjects for symbolic metamorphosis; and these, because of the magic power that binds the object to its image, are regarded as thaumaturgic 'carriers' capable of transmitting to their possessors the most favourable cosmic influences. This is the origin of the series of amulets which were thought of as condensers of such influences, and of the esoteric science connected with the making of them.

The objects concerned are often genuine works of art, small pieces of jewellery of exquisite craftsmanship. In other cases they may be formless, or almost formless, lumps, whose ability to radiate their power outwards beyond themselves derives from the material of which they have been made, as for instance the wood of a sacred tree. Amulets have always been of the first importance in all ancient civilisations, and particularly in ancient Egypt. Their influence extended during life and after death. In African civilisations recourse is usually made to them during a person's lifetime. They were a protection against illness; they promoted fertility and procreation; they warded off ill-luck; and they provided immunity against the slings and arrows of the enemy.

As has been noted earlier, the creative process entails the search for the symbol which will represent the radical archetypal element in which specific diversities are met. In this process, the invariable point of departure is naturalism; stylisation is the second or intermediate stage; and abstraction the third. But whichever of these stages prevails, the object itself will still reflect the collective vision of the group, while at the same time being stamped with the stylistic characteristics of the individual tribe. It is unnecessary and undesirable to look beyond 'stylistic centres' when we are judging the various works. Any attempt at further orientation would reduce us to the chop-logic of the museum catalogue that ignores the subsequent evolutions and developments taking place in the stylistic centres themselves.

The magnificent and ancient courts of Ife and Benin provide examples of decorative art not strictly connected with magic practices. But even here we should remember that iconography exalting the sovereign—surrounded by all the splendour of his court, or in the act of vanquishing his enemies—is nearly always the product of a species of magic insight, as is shown in similar iconography in ancient Egypt. It is the image that maintains and nourishes a connection with those forces that preside over earthly glory and feats-of-arms. The image is the receptacle of such forces, presaging the direction which future events will take.

Even in portraiture the artist does not shirk these canons, or conditions, but religiously fulfils his cult function. Admittedly, in the courts where artistic patronage was practised this function was more or less elastic. That is to say, there was always open to an artist the possibility of inserting elements of purely aesthetic value in his work. But here we are on another plane. In general, the creative process of the African artist is quite distinct from that of his Western counterpart. And we must take due account of this distinction in any comparative analysis, just as we must in making any 'objective' evaluation of what traditional Africa has bequeathed to us as her heritage.

5

THE SCULPTURE
PART ONE

Apart from the rock works, the oldest traces of artistic
activity on the Black Continent are provided by Bernard
Fagg's discoveries in Nigeria. These were made near the
village of Jaba and are known as the 'culture of Nok', the
word 'Nok' being the homonym of the actual region itself.
We know very little of the civilisation that produced these
works, which consist of a limited number of terracottas of
surprising artistic maturity. They are remarkable for the
way in which, in certain cases, they violate the canon of
'the front view' common to all African sculpture.

Finds similar to those at Jaba have also been made at
Jemaa, Wamba and Makafo, seats of the present Ham tribes.
The work is mostly naturalistic, though with a tendency to
formalism. There is, for instance, an interesting human
head in which the triangular eye-sockets are repeated in
the mouth which is shaped like a lozenge or double triangle
(Plate 6). The same excavations have also revealed a so-
called 'Janus Head'. These double-headed pieces are found
from Guinea to the Congo and are hermaphroditic in concept. There are also the remains of an ithyphallic statue,
originally 3 ft. in height, reflecting the same sort of ideas
about fecundity as we find in other African civilisations.
Examples of a naturalistic style occur in animal figurines
such as those of a seated monkey and of an elephant's
head; they are also found in representations of small
insects and vegetation elements, as well as in fragments of
human figures; and we find them in the sphere of personal
adornment, whether it be an elaborate head-dress, or a
bracelet, or a pearl necklace. In one fragment there is a

plastic quality about the curve of the leg that recalls Indian sculpture.

As for the date of these works, a geological survey of the strata in which they have been found places them with some probability in the middle of the first millennium BC. William Fagg calls this epoch 'siderolithic' because of the simultaneous presence of both stone and iron instruments.

The relics which constitute the 'culture of Nok' (perhaps the remains of objects once placed in votive shrines) have attracted the attention of scholars for the light they shed on prehistoric Africa. It is as though a bridge were thrown, from our day, across the oldest periods known to us, among which the culture of Ife, with its classical qualities, is outstanding. Can such a bridge ever reach firm ground on the farther shore? The answer rests in future discoveries.

IFE

The mystery surrounding the origins of the magnificent Ife culture stems from the time of Leo Frobenius's first discoveries there. Ife itself was the religious capital of the people of the Yoruba.

The strangest and most diverse theories have been evolved to explain both the general qualitative level, as well as the specific classicism, of Ife art which is so unlike what is found elsewhere in Africa. Frobenius related it to Plato's Atlantis; Delafosse perceived an Egyptian influence; other scholars deduce a possible Graeco-Roman contact. There has even been a suggestion that an Italian of the Renaissance was the moving spirit inspiring these magnificent art products; alternatively, the Portuguese Jesuits have been held responsible. There is something for all tastes. But the mystery remains.

A study of the Ife myths which recount the origins of the Yoruba group, and an examination of the techniques employed in the production of the actual objects themselves do, however, provide a few pointers. The myths teach us historical facts, although disguised as legend, while the various techniques reveal relationships with other cultures and possible sources of derivation.

As it happens, it is precisely in the city of Ife that we find traces of an extremely old cult related to the group's mythical origins. The central figure of this cult is the sea god, Olokun, who founded the Ife civilisation and implanted the ruling dynasty.

The Yoruba group were not alone among ancient people in conceiving that their civilisation came from the sea and was dependent on a sea entity. It was of course a conception that influenced the plastic traditions of later periods. It gave birth to images that epitomise the ideological elements in the myth by reinterpreting them not only in a particular historical context, but also in the light of stylistic canons which themselves result from the merging of diverse traditions. Thus we have, for instance, the plastic creation of an anthropomorphic being, the lower half of whose body is represented by the bi-forked tail of a fish.

Again, there is a wooden box of the Yoruba, preserved in Hamburg, on which is carved an anthropocephalic fish. It is the species known as *malapterus beniniensis*, and represents the mythical being in question. According to a later interpretation the myth centres on Ohen, the Oba of Benin in the fourteenth century, who—when his legs were paralysed—declared that he had been 'possessed' by the god Olokun.

Beroso relates a Babylonian myth which is somewhat similar. Again, civilisation comes from the sea. It is brought by a strange being, half man and half fish, called Oes or Oannes. He teaches the people agriculture, science and the arts by day, and returns to the sea in the evening. According to Beroso, Oannes was believed to have left a written record of the genesis of humanity; and the following passages from Beroso's rendering of it seem relevant to our enquiry:

'There was once a time in which there was nothing but darkness and an abyss of waters, wherein resided most hideous beings, which were produced of a twofold principle. . . . Men had one body, but two heads—the one of a man, the other of a woman. They were likewise, in their several orderings, both male and female. Other human figures were to be seen with the legs and horns of goats. Some had horses' feet; others had the limbs of a horse behind, but before were fashioned like men, resembling hippocentaurs. Bulls, likewise, bred there with the heads of men; and dogs, with fourfold bodies, and the tails of fishes . . . in short, there were creatures with the limbs of every species of animals. Added to these were fishes, reptiles, and serpents, with other wonderful animals, which assumed each other's shape and countenance. . . . The person who was supposed to have presided over them, was a woman named Omoroca; which in the Chaldee language is Thalatth; which in Greek is interpreted Thalassa, the sea: but, according to the most true computation, it is equivalent to Selene, the moon. . . .'

This extremely remote tradition—remote in place as well as time—has a direct relevance to our subject, otherwise we would not linger on it. To begin with, in both cases it is evident that the origins of civilisation were not autochthonous. Civilisation came from the sea: it was not a local product but the fruit of a sea-born race. And the record of this race has, with the passage of time, been divinised in myth. In fact, Beroso says that after the first Oannes many others (i.e. colonisers like Oannes) followed. Colonisation in Babylonia took place in successive waves, although at such a remote epoch that historical fact is merged in myth. And this myth operates syncretically as a plastic ideogram, epitomising the event. It was for this reason that the anthropomorphic image, recording the advent of the colonisers, took the form of the body of a fish, a fitting symbol of the mode of their arrival.

Similarly, in the civilisation of Ife, we are forced to recognise, at least in the matter of origins, an external impulse. But Beroso's account is also of particular importance in the more general tradition of mankind's genesis. In this first era we encounter hermaphroditic human beings with both male and female heads, and male and female sex organs. We also come across hybrid monsters whose forms comprise a medley of the characteristics of various animals —and this does not include solely the centaurs or satyrs of classical tradition.

A similar vision of the primaeval world is also found in many parts of Africa. We have already observed the so-called 'Janus Masks' which have double heads, one male and the other female. The Cameroons is the centre of a wide and varied iconography, which includes images with the organs of both sexes. Besides this there are, as we saw earlier, memories of monsters, centaurs and satyrs in the frescoes of the rock works (Plates 4, 5, and Drawing 3). Moreover, syncretism and hybridism have left definite traces on both the masks and sculptural works. In Owo art, a comparatively unknown offshoot of the Yoruba tradition, related to ancestor worship, or in Guro work, which is rather more sophisticated, anthropocephalic productions are decorated with the horns of totem animals (Plate B). Thus various ornaments such as horns, tusks, etc., proper to the masks of different tribes, perpetuate the cosmic vision of beings who, while retaining a human body, assume characteristics of the animal world.

We should, however, beware of assuming a direct connection between Babylonian civilisation and the civilisations of Africa. Apart from anything else, there is the insurmountable problem of chronology. But this vision of the world is something that Babylonia and Africa have in common. And in Africa the vision had a plastic dynamism that oriented men's minds towards the production of future manifestations.

Art therefore re-fashions and re-enacts the drama of creation. By breaking the seal of individuality it projects consciousness into that original sea in which the germs of all things have their being. The leader of the *corps de ballet*

27. Detail of stone statue. Full height about 2 ft. 4 ins.
The Sacred Grove of Esie, Nigeria.

28. Statuette in steatite (*nomori*). Height 1 ft. 3 ins. Mendi, Sierra Leone.

29. Fragment of sculpture in granite. Height 1 ft. 7 ins. Zimbabwe.

30. Statue in hammered copper, representing the god of war.
Height 3 ft. 6 ins. Dahomey.

31. Antelope with its young. Bambara wooden statue. Height
2 ft. 10 ins. French Sudan.

32. 'Motherhood'. Dogon wooden statue. Height 2 ft. 9 ins.

33. Senufo wooden mask.
Height 1 ft. 4 ins. Ivory Coast.

34. Senufo wooden mask with two faces. Height 11½ ins.
Ivory Coast.

35. Wooden statue of a woman. Senufo. Height 2 ft.
Ivory Coast.

36. Mendi statuette of a woman. Height 1 ft. 9 ins.
Sierra Leone.

37. Baule statuette of a woman. Height 2 ft. 1 in.

in this sarabande is Selene, the moon. As in the Oannes tradition, so in Africa she presides over the plane on which beings who are 'produced by a twofold principle' are said to exist.

These are the essential *motifs* in the mythical interpretations of human genesis. But they are not of themselves sufficient to explain the classicism of some of the Ife carvings, unless they suggest a foreign source as providing the initial impulse; but such an impulse cannot be singled out from the other elements of the substrate of which it is a part. It is in itself solely that the art of Ife—born possibly of external forces—finds the impulse to maintain and develop its tradition. The face of Lajuwa, the legendary usurper of the throne of Ife, has a purity that is almost Hellenistic (Plate 7), and this purity, this aristocratic detachment, forms a common denominator between the various bronze and terracotta pieces.

Sometimes, facial scarification in the form of geometric *motifs* exalts the values of 'plastic transitions', determining a subtle play of vibrant *chiaroscuro* (Plate 8). It is difficult not to relate some of the pieces to ancient Egyptian art. It is not only the abstraction—even though there is a naturalistic basis to this in the faces of African statues—but something of the same sense of holiness that evokes the Pharaonic world. In fact, a scintilla of hieratic Egypt lives again in the works of Ife.

Exactly how and when Egyptian influence made itself felt is still uncertain. It is true that Delafosse has revealed traces of it in the Sudan, extending as far as the Ivory Coast; and William Fagg is of the opinion that the Yoruba may have known the Egyptian technique of working bronze before they left the regions of the Upper Nile. This migration would have taken place in the first century AD, and may well have come in contact with the late Graeco-Nubian civilisation of Moeroe. If this theory is true, it would explain the appearance of the germ of classical realism—even if in decadent form—in the archaic art of Yoruba; and it would be just this influence of realism which, transplanted to Guinea, was developed there in such individual ways in later periods. While this is certainly no more than a hypothesis, it is nevertheless one that should be taken into account.

We have said that, side by side with myth and legend, it is necessary to make a close study of the actual techniques used. In this way one may be able—albeit hypothetically—to establish comparative relationships and trace possible lines of derivation. The Ife bronzes, which consist of nineteen heads, and a bust of a king, were all worked by means of *cire perdue*, a technique used in all Benin work as well as by the Yoruba.

The method itself comprises various stages, and was demonstrated to P. A. Talbot as late as 1921 in Benin. First the artist moulded the rough outlines of a clay support; this was then coated with wax which was moulded in detail; next an envelope of clay was laid over the whole, with an opening into which the molten metal was poured. The metal dissolved both the wax and the clay support, receiving the impression which the former had left on the clay envelope. The final stage consisted of first removing the internal residua together with the envelope, and then scraping, polishing and daubing the piece to give it a good surface.

In 1910, a Yoruba sculptor called Ali gave Captain R. S. Rattray a demonstration of this process; but however worth while the demonstration may have been *qua* demonstration, the end-product is technically defective, and inferior to the older works produced by this means (Plate 9).

The fact that the bronze productions of the Late Period in Egypt (Saitic-Persian) were all executed by *cire perdue*, supports the idea of Egyptian influence in Ife; and the vehicle of this influence may well have been the migratory movements of the Yoruba from Meroe, for at this time bronze sculpture was at its peak.

Cire perdue, however, was not confined to bronze work. As we shall see, the goldsmiths of the Ivory Coast also used this method, developing it in their own way. Beyond this, it must follow, if we grant there was a current of Egyptian influence, that such an influence must have overlaid certain native ethnic elements. For instance, local traits emerge in the treatment of head-dress and beard in the bronze portraits. A series of small holes delineate the parts of the face where hair grows, serving to hold in place both the imitation head-dress and the beard (Plate 12).

This concept of an 'overlay' of influence is of considerable stylistic importance. It differentiates Ife work from whatever classical antecedents it may have had, while at the same time placing it firmly in its African context. In Egyptian statuary, the false beard, developed in Pharaonic times, was cast of the same metal as the rest of the statue: neither it, nor the head-dress, was ever made of organic materials, to be applied afterwards to the metal frame. Ifé statues are presumably portraits; and should there be sufficient evidence to connect them firmly with funerary practice, then the peculiar use of the head-dress and false beard composed of materials other than the statue, would emphasise the necessity of obtaining a living likeness—one might almost say an organic likeness—between the figure and its model. Apart from this, the Yoruba to-day still preserve the custom of reproducing the features of the deceased in their funerary statues.

The statue called *ako* was life-size, and the greatest possible care was taken in the treatment of the face, in order to identify the statue with the person represented. Statues such as the *ako* were used for the ceremony of the 'second funeral'. This consisted of a repetition of the obsequies performed at the original funeral, with due burial of the statue in lieu of the body. This is not the place to dwell on the magico-religious ideas at the root of this practice; but it is significant that, as William Fagg has shown, the naturalism of these funerary images is at least as great as that of the other Ife bronzes and terracottas.

Moreover, this life-like quality underlines another point

of contact with ancient Egypt. Anthropologically, the
faces represented in Ife statuary can be classified as belonging to:

A. the mythical race of Olokun;
B. the Moorish race;
C. the Obalufon-Egyptian race, who had a rounded
face-structure.

The importance of a division into types such as these is of
course relative between other categories. The examples
modulate between naturalism and stylisation. And there is
yet another category consisting of completely abstract
works which were nevertheless contemporary with the
realistic pieces. There can be no doubt of this contem-
poraneity since the abstract pieces come from the same
tomb as a terracotta head worked in a highly developed
and naturalistic style. The fact that widely divergent
styles can belong to the same period reveals yet another
aspect of the African mind; that is to say, the ability to
hold diametrically opposed principles without any apparent conflict or contradiction. In the present instance we
are not dealing with the evolution of a style, that is, with
matters of derivation and development. We are not even
concerned with products of different 'schools'. We are in
the presence of something more profound and radical. To
judge from the places where the pieces were found, as well
as from an analysis of the materials used, it would appear
that, in all likelihood, the same sculptor turned his hand
indifferently to realistic and to abstract work. It is important to emphasise that this 'reconciliation of opposites' has
nothing to do with Lévi-Brühl's 'pre-logical' state. It is,
rather, an expression of the many-sided morphology of the
African psyche which is capable of keeping its perceptual
experiences in watertight compartments, and of recreating
these experiences strictly in terms of the categories in
which they have been 'given'. In other words, every experience is drawn to its proper archetypal element, and the
phases of this process are (in the context we are considering)

perfectly logical and consistent—even though, from our Western Graeco-Roman point of view, there may be self-evident contradictions.

It is this faculty for reconciling opposites that especially distinguishes the art of Black Africa from that of Egypt. In Egypt the artist accepted the primacy of an artistic canon conceived of as being a reflection of ultimate Truth, or *Maat*. Plastic or pictorial expression of the artist's experience was held in the vice of this canon, which—being part of a universally accepted framework of ideas—precluded the expression of mutually contradictory principles. In his *credo*, and in his ability to conform to the laws of his artistic canon, the Egyptian artist achieves his end, in much the same way as a mathematician achieves his in the act of solving an equation.

This evaluation in depth has allowed us to trace the limits of possible Egyptian influence over the civilisations we are examining, which if it was ever a reality, was manifest in specific relationships such as those of aesthetic proportion, and in the diffusion of the method of casting bronze.

The finds at Tada, on the Niger, reveal a widespread diffusion of bronze statuary and are of a high plastic quality recalling both the terracotta fragments of Nok and the more supple elements in Indian sculptures. The most important of the Tada finds known as 'the seated person', does, it is true, suggest certain pieces of Egyptian statuary: the pose is not unlike that of the piece depicting the chief physician Ny-ankh-Ra; but the resemblance is incomplete because the African piece lacks the hieratic rigidity of the Egyptian.

The beginnings of Benin art stem from the classicism of the Ife tradition. There is a legend that in 1280 AD the fifth Oba, Oguola, of the race of the gods, commanded the Oni of Ife to despatch skilled artists to teach his people the art of casting bronze. This may well mark the beginning of the Benin bronzes, which bear the unmistakable stylistic imprint of the heads of Ife. Working solely on a stylistic basis it is possible to distinguish the following periods in Benin work:

A. the archaic period: from the beginnings to 1360;
B. the ancient period: from 1360 to 1500;
C. the period of development: from 1500 to 1575;
D. the period of maturity: from 1575 to 1648;
E. the period of renaissance: from 1648 to 1691;
F. the final period: from 1691 to 1819;

A classification such as this is not intended to have more than a somewhat limited historical value: it ignores subdivisions, evolutions within the same period, stylistic survivals, etc.

Morphologically, the statues of the oldest period show the contemporary influence of Ife. There is a figure of a dwarf, in Vienna, which displays certain derivative affinities with the VIth Dynasty statue of the Keeper of the Wardrobe, Khunumhotep, preserved in the Cairo Museum.

Benin art was almost exclusively concerned with the embellishment of the court. The sovereigns and personages of rank wore strands of coral necklaces piled about their necks, reaching up to, and almost covering, their chins. On top of this they loaded themselves with elaborate headpieces which were even capable of sustaining the added adornment of long, artistically carved elephant tusks, for the Benin artists were masters at carving in ivory. The necklaces had the magic value commonly attributed to coral. The well-known Princess's Head, in the British Museum, provides a fine example of this sort of self-adornment. The coral was sprinkled by the king with the blood of sacrificial animals during the periodical 'Festival of the Corals'; at the same time he pronounced the formula: 'O corals, when I adorn myself with you, endow me with wisdom and keep me apart from evil spirits and the spells of the witch-doctors.'

Some of the figures represented are full of an admirably expressive strength, particularly in the earliest period before the style had crystallised. The most characteristic products of Benin work were undoubtedly the celebrated ornamental plaques. As Dapper, the Dutch navigator, records in the description of his voyage published in 1686: 'The pillars of the royal palace were covered with brass plaques which were kept highly polished and which depicted the King's victories.' The fact that Dapper uses the word 'brass' for 'bronze' is presumably a fortuitous stroke of accuracy. Analysis of the metal has shown it to be alloy containing 90% copper with an addition of zinc. In the case of bronze the addition is of course of tin. The word 'bronze' has, however, become a part of the conventional terminology used to describe Benin work, and we must accept it as such.

The plaques show the King in peace and at war. In peace he is shown surrounded by his courtiers, who are servilely offering him their arms for support, or protecting him from the heat of the sun, using their shields as umbrellas. There are pictures of him at war, with sword uplifted, holding an enemy prisoner, while his warriors are bearing off the spoils of victory to a fanfare of horns and the roll of drums. As in Egypt, where the theme of the victorious sovereign was a common subject, the king himself was conventionally depicted on a larger scale than the rest. On other plaques, warriors are represented with their distinctive sword raised in threatening fashion. We also find images of the first Portuguese slave-traders, whose severed heads frequently appear on the plaques as decorative *motifs*, heavily bearded and hook-nosed.

Besides the plaques there are also groups of statuettes which develop the same themes, though with an emphasis on military subjects. There is an aggressive tension in the warriors, reinforced by the ornamental work on their armour, which often includes the savage *motif* of a chain of leopard's teeth. The possession of a tusk or claw was held to invest the owner—by means of the power of participation—with the aggressive qualities of the wild beast from which it had been taken (Plates 17 and 18). Apart from this, the leopard itself was sacred in Benin, and its effigy inspired many of the best artists in the city. If it was represented in isolation, it would be executed either in bronze or ivory. The mass of the body was compact and not without a certain elegance. The creature's spots, which were reproduced stylistically, achieved a luminous rhythmic effect of great plastic intensity. In Plate 19 the animal is shown set squarely on its four paws, erect, with a noble carriage. It is snarling, and its whole appearance is threatening. Plainly it is intended to symbolise the grandeur, power and glory of Benin.

Silhouettes of the leopard are often shown on the plaques (Plate 20); sometimes the heads appear in front view as in Plate 22. In examples such as this where two large heads are represented full-face, one above the other, one is particularly struck by the formalised naturalism of the style. As regards composition, the free space at the bottom of many of the plaques was worked with a burin, or chisel, in a stereotyped design of flowers and lanceolated leaves. Any space not so filled in was punctuated with minute holes. Von Luschan, a conscientious and learned classifier of the Benin bronzes, relates this practice to the well-known *horror vacui* shared by all primitive people. The chisels themselves were of tempered steel, and the technical mastery required to produce as well as use them is truly astonishing even to us to-day.

Another surprising detail concerning the Benin plaques is the striking contrast between the finely worked surface and the crude, uneven holes left for the nails. One theory, which seems to be the most likely and which is accepted by Segy, is that the plaques were originally fitted without nails into niches hollowed in the wooden pillars. At a later date, presumably between 1688 and 1710, invaders removed them and took them away as booty. They did not, however, take them overseas; and when in the eighteenth century they were recovered, they were again put to ornamental use; but this time they were nailed to the wooden pillars.

The deplorable state of most Benin work is due to the fact that it was eventually plundered by the British when,

PLATE B. Wooden mask of a man's head with the horns of an animal. Height 1 ft. 2 ins. Guro, Ivory Coast.

The Sculpture. Part One

in 1897, they sacked and burnt the city. In some of the pieces part of the bronze has melted; in others there are gashes caused by their being torn roughly from their places. These, and the burnt ivories, are the mute record of the city's rape.

The period of maturity, the peak of artistic production, occurred in the sixteenth century. It was due to the influence of a great artist, Ahammangiwa, who was probably of Hausa origin and was invited to Benin by the sixteenth Oba, Esigie. On the other hand, there are also traces of western influence, notably the torsion of the body in the statues of the first invaders.

The variety of Benin bronzes is very wide indeed. Von Luschan's enumeration in his *The Antiquities of Benin* runs to 2,400 pieces preserved in various museums, while in all more than 3,000 pieces are known to have been carried off from the capital. To-day, only a fiftieth of what was once to be seen remains in the place of its origin as part of the royal treasure of the present Oba of Benin.

The naturalistic style flowers in the figures of animals, winged creatures, fishes and crocodiles, etc. Plate 21 is a notably elegant example of such work. In its balanced composition of masses it seems an exquisite, almost 'Renaissance' piece. It is precisely this fine sense of balance that allows the chisel to unify the constituent elements of the piece so that no sense of their separateness remains.

Among the minor bronzes of Benin there is a special type of hand-bell used by worshippers before the Juju altar. Its distinctive sound was calculated to attract the spirit which was being invoked. The ancient custom of driving evil spirits away by ringing bells is related to the same order of ideas, although the object here was to repel rather than to attract. The ornamental work applied to these bells is of particular interest, since its main object was not aesthetic. The basic functional idea, common to shamanism everywhere, is that the power radiates from the form, and that the form is animated by its appropriate vibrations.

As Frobenius puts it: 'When the shaman beats his drum, on the front of which there is an image of the universe, he performs an allegory, evoking all the spirits of the sea, countryside, mountains and vegetable life.'

A study along these lines has not yet been applied to this type of bronze. There is, however, a hand-bell in the Segy collection engraved with a symbol shaped like a double spiral. We find a corresponding symbol in Egyptian iconography, and in that of Mesopotamia, where it is associated with Nintu, goddess of births. This fact could support the identification of the symbol on the Benin bell with the Egyptian hieroglyph *ḥmt*, the sign of the womb. The fellaheen to-day attach a metal reproduction of this symbol to the dried umbilical cord of a newly-born child. As such it is held to be a potent amulet.

Besides excelling in bronze, the Benin artist was also a master of ivory carving. He decorated elephant tusks with historical or mythological figures, always ensuring that the person of the sovereign was the centre-piece (Plate 23). These tusks were inserted in a bronze base, to form part of one of those heads which we have already described. Again, we often find reproductions of a leopard (Plate 24). The little stylised circles depicting the leopard's spots are painted in, providing an effective chromatic contrast with the clear ivory background. The human figures worked in ivory are not, in general, as fine as those in bronze, although there is a small mask which reveals an exquisitely expressive sensibility and a wonderful attention to detail (Plate 25). The various elements are perfectly balanced, from the decorative coral wound chastely and without undue extravagance round the chin, to the finely chiselled ears and the ornate head-piece embellished with miniature heads of European slave-traders—in themselves a clear indication of the time at which such works were produced.

Unfortunately the combined effects of atmosphere and termites have deprived us of examples of ancient wooden sculpture. With some possible exceptions, this applies throughout all Black Africa, where wooden masks and sculptures are not calculated to last more than about two centuries.

On the other hand, ivory has helped to preserve instruments used in ritual magic, besides ornamenting with various forms of complex symbolism such domestic articles as vessels, boxes, cups, and so on. There is an interesting late example of such work in a lid ornamented with a double head, preserved in the Ethnographic Museum in Rome (Plate 26). The base is decorated with two masculine and two feminine statuettes and has four cruciform elements supporting a plate, or platform, which in its turn supports the globular body of a sort of pyx.

There is a sentence from Von Luschan that provides a fitting close to our survey of Benin art which excels above all in bronze work: 'Cellini himself,' he says, 'could not have modelled better, nor anyone before or after him.'

ESIE

Esie is a village in Nigeria, in the province of Ilorin, sixty miles to the north-east of Ife, and its statues form an important part of the artistic patrimony of Black Africa.

A little way out of the village there is a glade in which a collection of 750 stone statues of various ages appear to be holding a sort of council. There are figures of both sexes, from 1 ft. 8 ins. to 3 ft. 6 ins. high, most of whom are seated on a mushroom-shaped bench. Phallic pillars connected with fertility rites are scattered among them. Beautiful girls with elaborate head-dresses and extravagant *parures* are seated beside meditative dignitaries each of whom holds a *rhyton* shaped like a horn. Some of the statues have facial scarifications, the fine-cut cicatrices elaborating a variety of patterns almost pictorial in their general effect. Others are crowned with tiaras and wear an expression of serene cheerfulness (Plate 27). All of them have the distinctive triple tattoo marks that run in parallel lines from the corners of the eyes towards the ears. The Yoruba call these

Tapa. They are related to the markings of the legendary leopard Agassu, totem of the royal family. The feminine curves of some of the pert girls' figures have been moulded in such a way as to recall the suave, supple lines of Indian sculpture.

According to local tradition the figures represent 'ancestors'. They were the object of a cult entailing the sacrifice of cocks whose blood was poured over the stone faces, gradually wearing them away. And it is to this, rather than to any atmospheric agency, that we must attribute their poor state of preservation. Yet it is still clear that the ancient artists took unusual care with the facial expressions and that the result is far from being just another example of stylistic hardening. The figures must, one feels, be genuine portraits, a fact which would accord with the theory that in their character as 'ancestors' they are connected with the Nupe kingdom. The historical records of this kingdom date from about AD 640. It was later conquered by the Yoruba, probably in the eleventh or twelve century. The kingdom once included Ife and Benin, and there are consequently traces of the artistic traditions of these centres, but related to a time before Yoruba influence began to make itself felt.

Such a large collection of sacred images, all dating from the same time, or at least from the same historical cycle, has led some people to believe that there must have been important inhabited centres nearby. The alternative— assuming that the figures are portraits of real people—is that their descendants had every single statue transported for distances varying from sixty miles in the case of Ife, to 180 in that of Benin. On the other hand, the elaborate *coiffures*, the necklaces, the charms, the ritual horn held in the hands of some of the figures, all point to a relatively advanced society in which some degree of pomp or ceremony was not lacking.

Only an archaeological survey of the region can hope to solve this problem; and it would be by going up the Niger towards Jebba, rather than downstream in the direction of Ife, that the most interesting discoveries would probably be made. Jebba is not far from Esie, and at Jebba a bronze statue of a warrior has been found with facial scarifications like those of the Esie 'ancestors' and with lips of the same shape, so that the likeness between the two is remarkable. There has been an effort to identify the Jebba warrior with Shango, the mythical king of the Yoruba. Meyerowitz, on the other hand, has discovered in it Nubian elements. Among these is the vulture ornamenting the front part of the helmet, a reference to the ancient Egyptian goddess Nekhebit. We shall return to this point in the next chapter.

The sacred glade of Esie is still a place of pilgrimage for the Yoruba, who keep the cult of the images alive with ritual sacrifices. Ancient tradition tells us that the spirits are evoked by ringing a small hand-bell of bronze.

SIERRA LEONE (MENDI)

Among the Mendi of Sierra Leone there are some curious stone statues which are related to what we must call the archaic cycle. They are scattered throughout the area in question, varying in height from 4 ins. to 6 ins. They are executed in steatite; they represent male and female figures; their heads are out of proportion to their bodies, being too large, while their pronouncedly prognathous features and frog-like eyes suggest the mythical hybrid creatures which represent man's transition from an animal to a human condition.

The Mendi themselves, who comprise most of the people of Sierra Leone, have totally different artistic traditions to those expressed in these statues. They are even ignorant of their origins, although they endorse their evident antiquity. The local name for them is *nomoli*, that is, 'people of steatite'. They turn up casually in the soil, and whoever finds one is held to be especially fortunate, for unusual and magical powers are attributed to them from their being in close contact with the world of spirits, over which they exercise authority.

For this reason they are placed in the rice fields under a little shelter of palm leaves. If the harvest is poor they are whipped. It is particularly important for women to keep well away from these statues since accidental contact with them might cause sterility.

The diminutive statuettes are mostly shown in a sitting posture. Their chins are cupped in their hands; their lips are large and swollen; their eyes are protuberant and they have enormously large ears. The masculine images are often ithyphallic, while a supple, plastic sensuality of the legs, reminiscent of Indian statuary, frequently characterises the female images (Plate 28).

Their use was interwoven with tribal life: they were used in court cases, witnesses having to swear by them. A false oath taken on one of them would expose the guilty party to the vengeance of those spirits dependent on that particular *nomori*.

Our ignorance of the civilisation that has produced these strange works is almost complete. We are unable to sketch even the barest outline of their history. If we except the bronze rings discovered in the same region as the *nomoli*, they do not seem to be associated with any other artistic manifestations. They stand alone.

SAO (CHAD)

The archaeological excavations of J. P. Lebeuf to the south of Lake Chad have revealed traces of an old civilisation established from the very earliest times in the Chari delta, and later—in the tenth century—rather more to the west, whence the people to whom this civilisation belonged were driven towards the close of the sixteenth century. They were called the 'Sao'. In terms of the ethnocentralism we examined in an earlier chapter the name means simply 'man'. They appear to have been composed of two groups: one dark skinned and the other fair skinned. Their descendants are believed to be the present Kotoko.

The Sculpture. Part One

They were skilful workers in clay, building their villages of this material, while their cult sites are full of votive statues in terracotta. In common with other ancient peoples, they placed the remains of their dead in terracotta jars.

The most important cult, if we may judge from the images in the sanctuaries, seems to have been ancestor worship. When a man died, his funerary mask was placed in the sanctuary. The cardinal points of the sanctuary were marked by symbolic clay spheres. These were presumably intended to ward off evil spirits. In ancient Egypt clay bricks, which were sometimes inscribed with the names of the four sons of Horus, were built into the walls at the cardinal points, with exactly the same aim.

A neolithic site, 187 miles to the east of Lake Chad, near Lake Fitri, appears to be the oldest in the region. South of Chad, at Tago, there is a sanctuary of particular importance in which have been found interesting clay masks and statues.

According to J. P. Lebeuf, these statuettes are ancestor images. They were used to attract the spirit or vital force, so that it would not disturb the living. The idea of a statue or stele 'housing' and 'absorbing' the spirit of the deceased was a part of the heritage of every ancient civilisation, and its use still survives in some areas in modern times.

Although the funerary images of the Sao resemble those of Egypt in the use to which they were put, they differ from them in the lack of any sense of portraiture. The Egyptians in their statue of the *Ka* took the greatest care to achieve as close a facial resemblance as possible between the image and its original. The Sao neglected this principle of identification.

The greater part of the figures fall into two groups: 'ancestors' and 'masked dancers'. They are worked in clay and are signalised by their lack of lower limbs; the tallest are 14 ins. high. The trunk is massive, accentuating the resemblance to a stele; the shoulders are wide and square, and the arms are shown in a gesture of 'offering'—an extremely rare attitude in African statuary. The head, however, is the most interesting part. It is more stylised than the rest of the figure: the lips are at once flat and protuberant, recalling those in some of the wooden masks, as well as those of some of the Sara women in the Ubanghi-Shari. The severity of the whole is accentuated by the formal resolution and reorganisation of the face in rising planes of almost brutal force. The top of the skull has a sort of superstructure of short stumps, in which various plumes were placed during religious ceremonies.

The statuettes of the 'masked dancers' are even more massive than those of the Esie 'ancestors'. They are clear evidence of the ritual use of masks among the Sao, the commonest images being those of the bull and goat.

The work in clay is associated with that in bronze, for the Sao excelled equally in both. They used the method of *cire perdue* to make ritual objects such as libation cups, necklaces, bracelets, breast-straps, and brooches. Among the animals reproduced in bronze are crocodiles, together with the head of a gazelle, and these are better executed than their clay counterparts. The ornamental *motifs* consist of undulating lines and double spirals such as we have seen reproduced on the bronze bell of Benin and which recur on Ashanti pieces.

Sao art came to an end in the sixteenth century, when the Moslems arrived in the region. This event is the cause of numerous problems which are as much to do with the highly personal style of the sculpture as with the actual bronze industry itself. The very existence of this was unsuspected until the recent discoveries were made. Unquestionably, the majestic massiveness of the images, their sense of volume and the resolution and reorganisation of the various facial elements—quite apart from the ritual aspect which in fact constituted their vital substrate—render Sao works among the most significant in African civilisations.

38. Baule statuette of a woman. Height 1 ft. 3½ ins.

39. Baule ancestor image. Height 1 ft. 3½ ins. Ivory Coast.

40. Baule wooden mask. Height 1 ft. 3 ins. Ivory Coast.

41. Wooden mask of an elephant-man figure, with brass ornamentation. Height 1 ft. 3½ ins. Baule, Ivory Coast.

42. Wooden image promoting fecundity (*Akua-ba*). Height 1 ft. 1 in. Ashanti, Ghana.

43. The 'Lady with the double axe'. Yoruba wooden sceptre. Height 1 ft. 8 ins.

44. Ritual instruments (*edan*) in bronze. Heights: 1 ft. 2½ ins. and 1 ft. 3½ ins. Yoruba, S. Nigeria.

45. Anyang mask of wood covered with skin. Height 1 ft. 5 ins.
Southern Cameroons.

46. The throne of the king of the Bekom. Wood, with ornamentation in copper and polychrome glass beads.
Height 5 ft. 10 ins.

47. Girl's head in wood, with a wig. Height 11 ins. Southern
Cameroons.

DAHOMEY

The Abomey and the Fon constitute, together with part of the Yoruba, the population of Dahomey. They are the heirs of an ancient military kingdom recorded by Leo Africanus, that had a battalion of Amazons.

A complex pantheon, rich in zoomorphic divinities, inspired the production of statues and masks, some of which will be examined in the next chapter. The process of *cire perdue* links the bronze statues with the oldest cycles. Their ability to express dramatic tension in bronze is exemplified in a unique piece representing the god of war (Plate 30). In Dahomey, an original technique was developed which consists of covering wooden statues with bronze or silver plates.

The Abomey above all developed the art of bas-relief in wood or clay, treating individual rather than grouped subjects: human figures, animal *motifs* and vegetation elements. As in Benin, so in Dahomey, art was essentially supported by and directed towards the court: it had a precise sociological end. It certainly reflected ritual conceptions, but it was also ornamental, embellishing the royal palace and the houses of state dignitaries. Articles of household use, clothing, etc., were also objects of the minor arts. This tradition was not only maintained by the vitality of religious conceptions, but also by the demands of the court, and its end coincided with the eclipse of the monarchy. In Chapter 9 we shall detail the crucial points in the artistic crisis which attended the decline of the African courts, together with the elements that survived and the possible lines of development.

ZIMBABWE

We have already given a summary sketch of the civilisation of Zimbabwe in the chapter on the rock works. Here we shall only note the possibility of stone sculpture having later developed side by side with the magnificent architecture. The example of Zimbabwe work produced here represents a headless vulture clutching an elk in its talons (Plate 29). It is interesting to observe the different treatment of the two creatures: the bird of prey is executed in the round, while the elk is worked in bas-relief.

Other sculptures of the vulture have been found in the same area. It is shown hovering above a high pole. The pole is sometimes phallic and looks like a totem symbol. The manifest maturity, technically and stylistically, is astonishing. Scholars who have associated these works with so-called 'Bushman art' are plainly in error.

Although some of the objects that have come to light in the same neighbourhood have been attributed to the fourteenth century, there is as yet insufficient evidence to allow us to date any of the finds with any certainty. It seems, indeed, most likely that they were produced about the time of the archaic cycle of Zimbabwe, thus permitting the influence of other civilisations, such as that of Egypt, to make itself felt. The iconography of the vulture and especially of the falcon on the top of a pole was common in Egypt up to the end of the predynastic era.

6

THE SCULPTURE
PART TWO

Wood and ivory have always been the media in which the
African artist has found his most perfect plastic expression.
From the earliest times he has shown a preoccupation with
the intrinsic nature of his material, as is plain from the
products themselves, whether they be ancestor images,
magic statues, masks, amulets, thrones, ritual instruments
or objects of domestic use.

The complex symbolism of the tree is common to the
oldest cycles, and the ideas inherent in the sanctity of the
tree live again in many of these pieces. The tree represented a universal cosmic force which conferred immor-
tality; it was the symbol of the vertical, upward thrusting
power of the male; besides which it had the faculty of
harbouring potent spirits of nature. Consequently, since
the power of the whole is manifest in the part, the wooden
image will possess the force of the tree from which it has
been taken as well as all the powers attributed to the idea
of trees in general by that particular civilisation. The same
principle is applicable to ivory, whose use was, however,
confined to regions inhabited by elephants. In the case of
ivory, 'participation' does not transmit any specific sacred
power, but rather qualities such as might, indomitable
courage, aggressiveness, longevity, which are the distinctive
characteristics of the species.

Thus both wood and ivory were considered as harbouring
the vital force, *nyama*. They were a sort of epicentre for its
outward, radiating impulse. The direction this impulse
should take was determined by the form which the wood
or ivory had been given by the sculptor, which would itself

conform to certain traditional stylistic canons or, alternatively, to some individual, if group, vision of the suprasensible world. The sculpture was therefore a plastic ideogram, a part of the strange 'theatre of the psyche' where the visions of the roots of things operate and have their being. Hyperconsciousness, naturally or artificially induced, tends to establish contact with forces latent in the psyche, and is subsequently destined to achieve identification with them by dramatising their essence on the plane of visions of the suprasensible. From this point of view, the sculptor is a magician, or at least a witch-doctor, and as such is the object of veneration, fear and, in some tribes, of aversion. Depending on the attitude of the tribe to his profession, so he belonged from the beginning to a certain social rank or caste.

The most outstanding characteristic of African sculpture, from a strictly structural point of view, is the intentional deformation to which, in comparison with its model in the real world, the image is submitted. It is as though convex or concave mirrors had distorted the artist's vision of reality. We see disproportionately large heads on small bodies; elongated torsos; lower limbs that have been reduced to a minimal size, or else blown out in an exaggerated rotundity. The sphere and the cube are refracted, resolved, re-composed, continually investing the surface concepts of the artist with extraordinary vitality.

African sculpture tends to be functional and severe, to express what is essential. It creates a set of terms each of which is intended fully to define a single idea. The more this definition can be stripped of circumlocutions and irrelevancies and stick to a just interpretation of reality, the more vital such terms will be. And this principle is realised in the sculpture. Here the plastic ideogrammic value lies in the fact that it is the formal analogue of the conceptual content. The constituent parts of each term are comprised of structural co-ordinates of a spatial nature whose interpretation by the observer takes place on the emotional level. Since the same idea can be expressed in different terms, each one reflecting the substrate of the individual artist, the plastic ideogram—although manifesting the same order of ideas—can vary in its formal expression from tribe to tribe. As evidence of this may be cited the rise of particular styles (sometimes related to distant prototypes) that have become a part of local tradition, while at other times an individual elaboration is expressed in the language of the group.

We have still to show that the term 'pre-logical' is inapplicable to the African sculptor, and that his products are more than manifestations of arrested childhood. A child's products are not directed to a goal that the spirit has envisaged from the beginning. The child does not look to science—even though its methods may be empirical—in order to obtain a specific end. But African 'art' work *is*, on the contrary, the fruit of a perfectly logical process, one that appears consistent within the framework of its own mental orientation. The African sought to produce an object that, by virtue of specific rules, might achieve the end implicit in such rules. Whether one believes in these rules or not is irrelevant in assessing their logicality. For the African they constitute an intensely lived *credo*, and their logicality can be judged only in relation to the antecedent and subsequent terms in the artistic process itself. This is the most important point in any consideration of African statuary.

The sculptor's rudimentary instruments are evidence of a genuine primitiveness. He used the small chopper, various types of knives, pincers, needles, etc. Only a consummate skill, capable of transmitting a part of the sacred fire to the instrument, can explain the intensity of some of the end products. It is no small thing to create an image. It is a rite that has its beginnings in the search for the very materials themselves. There is the choice of the tree from which the block of wood is to be taken; the block has to be roughly shaped at the place where it is cut; if the work is being done for a third person, then the 'client' also must be present; finally, there are invocations to accompany the various acts. All this shows how different the creative process was for an African artist when compared with a European. It must of course be understood that this applies only to the cultural cycle preceding the arrival of Europeans in Africa, or to the few places that still preserve an unbroken link with the old traditions.

African artists prefer to work with wood that is still fresh and soft. They avoid hard substances. This is partly due to the sort of instruments they use, and partly to the importance they attach to the vital fluid still present in a fresh block of wood.

The real work of the sculptor, however, as we can observe in isolated cases even to-day, begins in the artist's hut after he has made an offering or sacrifice to whatever spirit is believed to be connected with the projected object. The block gradually takes shape under the hands of the craftsman. The proportions of the parts assume a rhythmic relationship; details emerge and are refined. If a traditional model is being copied, then the process takes longer than it would for an original piece. This process continues until the work has been completed. Finally, there follow the daubing and greasing with vegetable substances to create a surface finish. Mineral pigments mixed with grease are sometimes used; or the piece is soaked in various coloured dyes and then left to dry in the sun; sometimes lamp-black is used. Such procedures are tribal 'trade secrets'. The precise nature of the surface finish is determined by the vegetable or mineral products found in the area; and, it should be added, these techniques are used for ivory as well as wood. The greasing which the object undergoes, its frequent use and consequent contact with the skin, add to the intensity of the original patina, lending the piece an aesthetic value intrinsically in accord with our Western notions. If the image, whether a statue or mask, is a cult object, it will from time to time have ritual liquids poured over it, such as the blood of sacrificial victims, milk, etc., which further modify its surface colouring.

With masks, the patina is often replaced by a polychrome

design in tempera obtained from a mixture of coloured clays and a sort of gummy, watery substance. In this case, if the mask is in frequent use the colours are retouched from time to time so that they will keep their original brilliance. Even here our evaluation is independent of the ritual *virtu* of the painted drawings on the mask. The various uses to which the masks are put call for special colours. Thus, in summoning spirits and in the rites of the dead, the colour is white, since it is believed that this is the colour assumed by ghosts at night. Our own mental associations are the fruit of a world that is totally foreign to the Negro. When confronted with a work of African 'art' we evoke ideas of beauty, of the grotesque or the horrible, where quite other reactions were originally looked for. The ideas of civilised European man are foreign to the plastic African ideogram; and it is therefore scarcely surprising that a mask which he finds merely horrible should in fact be part of a ritual dance in which it was intended to reduce the participants to helpless laughter.

The African artist reflected reality in the distorting mirror of his own spirit. He also consistently applied certain rules such as that of the 'frontal' view in statuary. This, together with the asymmetrical division of the two parts of a statue by means of vertical planes, invests much of the work with an air of calm serenity.

Another outstanding feature of African statuary is the head. This is often out of all proportion to the rest of the body. Sometimes the object in question is simply an isolated head; but even if this is not so, the emphasis still falls on that part of the body. This is due to the particular importance paid to the 'seat of thought', even extending after death in the cult of ancestor skulls. A man's individuality is concentrated in his head. This is so firmly felt that in some rites the other organs are often ignored altogether. The idea recalls the use of the so-called 'reserve head' found in the necropolis of Ghiza in the Old Kingdom of ancient Egypt. Heads were preserved in the *serdab*, the receptacle where the statue of the *Ka* was kept. Even if the statue itself was destroyed, the head alone would fulfil the function of the entire image. The presence of the deceased could manifest itself in the skull, where part of its essence came to life again. The ritual cups in use among various ancient civilisations are related to this order of ideas. They consist of paternal skulls, since it was held that the drink poured into them was impregnated with hereditary forces, preserving a bond of communion with the ancestors. One of the commonest types of cup used by the Bakuba is strictly linked to this conception.

Among some tribes, such as the Baule, the treatment of the face constitutes a real piece of portraiture, whose aesthetic value is derived from that of the subject. But these are exceptional cases. Mostly we find ourselves confronted with stylised forms. Identification with a specific individual, as in the case of ancestor images, is effected by the witch-sculptor's ritual naming of the image. Such statues perpetuate the memory of a dead person and sometimes also serve to 'absorb' his spirit, and so prevent its inconveniencing or harming the living.

Images made on the death of one or both of a pair of twins are particularly widespread among the Yoruba. These images, called *ibeij*, are treated as living beings. They are fed daily with food such as the yoke of an egg, and afterwards their faces are washed. The equivalent of the Egyptian statue of the *Ka*, intended to house the shade of the deceased, is in use among the greater part of the peoples of Africa under the name of *ndozzi*. The widow weeps before it in words similar to those used by the 'wailers' in Pharaonic times:

'Woe, woe is me! I have lost him whom I loved, my joy! He who delighted me with his words, who cheered me with his looks, is no more! Unhappy me! What will become of me? Cruel spirits, you who have snatched him from me, set death in my path! Guardian spirits of my beloved, guardian spirits of your suppliant, give him to me again, since I am in death's way, since I am already dead!'

PLATE C. Wooden mask of the Dan. Height 9 ins. Liberia and Ghana.

The Sculpture. Part Two

The words of grief have a spontaneous lyricism. The African does not suffer from self-critical inhibitions. He stands before an omnipresent nature and, as though by reflex, habitually gives vent to the maximum potential of his feelings. Love, hate, sorrow, suffering, all are deeply felt, all are sustained at the most intense level, spontaneously permeating not only personal behaviour but all artistic expression. The magic statue designed to harm an enemy and pierced with hundreds of nails is saturated with the hate which has been lavished on it. The meditative images of the grandparents among the Fang, reflect a vein of melancholy. And the African ideal of fecundity inspires the innumerable 'mother' images: the mother suckling her child is a common theme in all African iconography, albeit subject to stylistic variations.

What we should call artistic productions are found solely among the agricultural peoples, and the higher the agricultural level, the higher the level of their 'art' products. The nomadic hunters have produced nothing, a fact indicative of the formative influence which agriculture has on a people's character. Frobenius has shrewdly summed up the essence of this influence as follows: 'I have been asked under what conditions the life of the African realised itself most fully. I think in the farmer's way of life. . . . It is he who persists: the spirit of the farming race is not to be trampled underfoot. Therefore I say that the nature of the Africans is best reflected in the farmer. You are mistaken if you believe that the great cities, the nobility of town-dwellers, the power of the great emperors and kings, do not bear the imprint of an agricultural race. It is the emperor who breaks the first furrow; the manual work is farmers' work; the art is the art of a farming people; the aristocracy has its roots in farming. And, above all, their expressions of joy reflect the interests of a farming people. . . .'

The three phases of naturalism, stylisation and abstraction are exemplified in both wood and ivory sculpture. More than this, vital examples of each often appear at the same time and in the same object. We are again confronted with the problem of varying styles and the evolution of set types of pieces. Grave physical difficulties, however, prevent our arriving at a satisfactory formulation of the problem. Wood is the least durable of materials used, incapable of withstanding the combined effects of climate and of termites. Unless the object has been preserved in a suitable place and subjected to constant greasing, it cannot be expected to last very long. The pieces in museums rarely go back before the eighteenth century, most of them bearing scant indications of their origin. Moreover, colonisation and the struggle against 'paganism' waged by various missionaries, have for the most part resulted in the decline of indigenous art forms and in the systematic destruction of all so-called 'idols'. Only recently, Father Spiritain, a missionary in Gabon, announced that he had succeeded in burning more than 6,000 such pieces.

On the other hand, ritual objects were often destroyed by the craftsmen themselves, once they had fulfilled their function. This was the case with the individual masks used in circumcision rites. The origins of the use of masks are lost in the mists of time. Ibn Batuta, the Arab chronicler, records that he used to assist at masked dances in the Sudan in 1352. But between then and now forms have changed. New styles have evolved under pressure of the migrations of peoples, of wars and the imposition of foreign cults. It would appear all but impossible to trace an overall pattern in such confusion extending over so long a period. Our only firm guide are the so-called 'secret societies'. These were common to all tribes, their function being eminently that of conservers of tribal tradition. In his study of the subject, Capt. F. W. Butt-Thompson has emphasised this point in a passage quoted by Underwood. He says that such societies were formed to strengthen and preserve tribal traditions, customs and beliefs that ran the risk of modification or decadence. Such organisations were champions of the old as opposed to the new, and this is still the case with some of their descendants. He goes on to say that they set the limits of the tribe's mental horizons, punishing heretics and any who did not conform to the norm. He says that they were intelligent enough, however, to see that prohibition alone would be an inadequate basis for a society intended to last for any length of time; and that they therefore made their societies the sanctuaries of legends, myths and history, of artistic and cultural conceptions, of the tribe's conscience and its wisdom—in short, of the entire tribal patrimony. In addition, they made themselves the transmitters of all this knowledge, becoming in effect the sole teachers of tribal matters.

It was in this way that particular styles, the heritage of remote predecessors, managed to survive, although it is not always possible for a tribe to draw on such a source. The separate societies, numerous as the tribes themselves, were based on rigid disciplinary rules. Capital punishment hung like a sword of Damocles over the heads of their members. Total secrecy shrouded their rites. Sometimes these rites consisted of cruel or bloody practices. They were invariably rooted in ritualistic magic and tribal policy. Indeed, the societies derived their influence from the fact that it was they who imposed the law proper to the tribal potentate or government. In a word, they were the *custodes custodium*.

These societies were mainly male, although corresponding female associations were quite common. In the more degenerate forms the members bound themselves by ritual witchcraft so that they became 'leopard-men,' etc. In the higher forms it is indisputable that they have exercised a beneficial influence, whether in conserving tribal traditions or controlling the despotism of the chiefs. Many of them resisted European occupation; and although they have lost a lot of their real power, they still retain a certain influence over their members. We shall deal with them more fully from the artistic point of view when we come to examine the masks and ritual instruments of the various tribes.

Apart from the problem of dating, and that of morphological evolution, there remains the classification of the various styles, a problem that fairly bristles with difficulties. It is perfectly true that one can identify certain 'centres of style': Carl Kjersmeier based his work on this principle, saying: 'A true picture of African sculpture is to be obtained not by continuing, as at the present time, to speculate in a general way on the different art forms, but by a radical examination of the various stylistic centres; that is, by an examination of the art of a large number of Negro peoples who have reached that pitch of artistic development which permits the rise of specific styles.'

J. C. Pauvert is opposed to this theory. He writes: 'It is unsatisfactory because it treats African forms solely from the outside, being satisfied with a temporal significance that is itself pseudo-historical and aesthetic, and which makes an abstraction of African beauty. . . . This theory is another example of the way the West has fabricated the idea of African art. The "centres of style" derive more from museum studies than a genuine aesthetic analysis.'

These two statements reveal the conflict of views prevailing among scholars. Both observations are just. Kjersmeier's proposed classification holds good for us as spectators; but the limits of such a classification are indicated by Pauvert's denial of its *objective* validity. Pauvert's spectator is in the position of one who belongs to an African culture; and in support of Pauvert, we have already observed the divergence between our Western aesthetic appraisal of an African 'art' product, and that of its creator.

From yet another point of view, the dialogue on the subject of African art can be seen to be a monologue. Western theories cannot correspond with those of the original artist whose aim, stylistically, was to execute a series of variations on specific forms. Nor can his views correspond with those of the artist's descendants, whose contacts with Europeans have profoundly affected all their mental attitudes. Would it be possible for Western man to recreate the African's early world, and by an act of empathy to experience it emotionally within himself, evoking again the original emotion of the African artist? This is technically impossible, for he belongs to another culture cycle, the determinant of a psychic substrate intrinsically different from that of the African. The impossibility of performing such an act of empathy underlines the subjectivity of our judgements in relation to African art. It is a vicious circle from which there would appear to be no escape.

The only possible solution would seem to lie in a deeper understanding of the life and habits of the various Negro peoples. In this way we shall acquire a knowledge of the exact end and purpose of each object: we shall be able to identify the subsistent motives prompting their creation. It is necessary to place ourselves, by an intellectual effort of the imagination, in the position of the African artist in order to achieve a sympathetic understanding of his artistic process. In this field the contribution of an intelligent and lively ethnography would be invaluable. With greater knowledge, and by a conscious identification with the creative processes of a civilisation foreign to us, we may hope to dislodge the purely subjective elements in our aesthetic evaluation.

As far as classification is concerned, even the best method has an entirely relative value—a value, that is, related exclusively to us. The most rewarding approach is to be found in a study of the external formal elements and of the affinities and contrasts between them. Although we must still bear our relativistic premise in mind, from this point of view, the so-called stylistic centres provide a useful method of approach and, as such, can be fully utilised. Lavachery based himself on just such external formal elements, region by region, concentrating his attention on the head of the statue. He has proposed a two-style classification: the 'concave' and 'convex'. In the first case, the block of wood used by the artist has been hollowed in such a way that the nose and eyes and, sometimes, the mouth, are carved in what is left of the wood after the hollowing.

In the convex style, such features as eyes, nose and mouth, are superimposed on a rounded facial surface.

The following is Lavachery's classification:

Concave style:
The people of the Sudan: Habbe, Malinke, Bobo, Bambara, etc. The people on the north-east borders of the ex-Belgian Congo: Azande, Momvus, Manghbetu of Ituri (whose contours are already rounded owing to the influence of their neighbours).
In the south-east: Warega (of the Bantu group).
In the west: Senefo, Baule, Guro of the Ivory Coast, Fang and Bakota of Gabon.

Convex style:
People of the Atlantic coast, from Liberia to the south of the Province of Benguela.
People of the central savannahs of the Cameroons and of the Congo Basin, of the regions of the Great Lakes, and the Kasai.
In the interior: Baluba, Basongo, Balunda, etc.

I propose in the following pages to examine, at least in outline, the various styles of African art. The nature of this study requires that we keep ourselves within certain limits. What follows, therefore, is not intended to be simply a table of names and terms, any more than it is an exercise in the vaguely exotic. There would be no difficulty in drawing up hundreds of names of tribes and sub-tribes. The reader would be bombarded by a seemingly endless recurrence of strange names which, in the result, would shed more confusion than light. The *raison d'être* of this volume presupposes a contact, or communication, on the human level far removed from arid schemes of classification. We shall thus cite the stylistic centres one by one on a regional basis, and, by means of illustrative plates, shall relate the art objects themselves to their original uses and to the various conceptions connected with the African artistic process.

The Sculpture. Part Two

As we shall be listing the names of many of the tribes it may be as well at this point to draw attention to the principle of ethnocentric separatism. We have already mentioned this earlier; it characterises every race, identifying each with the people *par excellence*. We shall indeed often find the prefix *Ba* or *Bu* which signifies, precisely, 'people'. Thus Baluba is equivalent to 'People of Luba', referring to the mythical chieftain, Luba. The Bushongo are the 'People of the knife *shongo*', a warlike instrument with multiple blades. It is an extremely functional weapon, although somewhat abstract in form. It was thrown from an ambush, whence (revolving) it would flash like lightning and cut off the enemy's legs. The Baluba, to whom this instrument was unknown, called the Bushongo, who used it, 'Bakuba'—that is, 'People of the lightning'; and it is under the second name that the Bushongo are currently known. Individuals, on the other hand, are denominated by the prefix *Mo* or *Mu*. For example, Baluba is the name of the people and Muluba of one who belongs to that group.

Philologists tend to detach the prefix from the rest of the name. Thus they write Ba-Luba for Baluba, etc. Although it is true that this method admits of greater scientific precision, it is better to retain the traditional and widely accepted orthography. We shall not ignore the results of recent studies, however, when these entail significant variations. The monthly publication, *Le Livre Africain* (Brussels, March 1959), has, for instance, proposed the spelling 'Kongo' for the ex-Belgian Congo, Mu-Kongo to designate an individual of the Ba-Kongo group, Mu-Luba for an individual of the Ba-Luba group, etc.

Let us begin our survey by travelling from north to south along the West African coast. The first people we meet are those of the ex-French Sudan, among whom are the Bambara of Mali, a tribe of 750,000 members, who are of ethnographic as well as numerical importance. They are a race of farmers firmly attached to the land all the year round, and more particularly at the time of their ritual

91

dances at the beginning and end of the farming season. The tribal insignia is the antelope, an animal once lord of the forests. It forms part of their ritual dances either as a head-piece or as the upper part of the mask. The imaginative and technical ability of the Bambara is well displayed in these carved images called *sogoni-kun*, representing Tji-wara—that is, the great and small antelopes, whose names are respectively *Dajde* and *Sogoni*.

The virtuosity of the artist has resulted in an elegantly stylised effect. The periphery concentrates a vital tension, conferring on the piece an autonomous life, the sense of a spring which is about to be released, and which corresponds to the taut quality of the animal itself (Plate 31). The dancers fasten the *sogoni-kun* to their heads by means of thongs, cushioning it on a support of straw. They then proceed to imitate the movements, the leaps and bounds, of the animal, by which they are supposed to be psychically possessed. It is an affirmation of the supremacy of the ancient totem sign of the region, and at the same time an assimilation and harnessing of the vital forces scattered over the fields. This dance is held whenever a new piece of ground has to be ploughed and cultivated.

Apart from the innumerable variations devised by the sculptors of different centres on their basic models, *Dadje* and *Sogoni* are also differentiated according to sex. The male model is larger, and the animal is reproduced with its mane, which allows for a play of light on the geometrical forms of wood inlay. Stylisation and abstraction lend a formal purity to the whole. Any suspicion of over-elaboration is totally lacking, even in specimens that carry a multiple superstructure—an element that might plainly lend itself to a decadent ornateness. The various pieces are modelled on a dynamic rather than a static principle. They reproduce in wood that potential force you see in an animal—momentarily immobile, but on the point of swift movement.

The female model is simpler and, lacking the mane, lacks also the geometrical designs of the male model. On its back it carries a young antelope, an indication of its maternal

48. Duala polychrome wooden mask. Height 1 ft. 5 ins.
Southern Cameroons.

49. Abu poly-
chrome wooden
mask. Height 3 ft.
Cameroons.

50. Bakota funerary image. Wood covered with hammered
bronze. Height 2 ft. 1 in. French Congo.

51. Banku wooden throne. Height of the seat: 1 ft. 8 ins.; of the figure seated on it: 1 ft. 7 ins. Cameroons.

52. Bangu-Bangangte demon in wood painted red and white.
Cameroons.

53. Top of a Kuyu polychrome wooden mask. Height 2 ft. 5 ins.

54. M'Pongwe polychrome wooden mask for a woman (white, red and black). Height 1 ft.

55. Wooden sculpture with copper ornaments. Height
1 ft. 1 in. without the base. Pangwe, Gabon.

attributes and, by reflex, of the idea of fecundity always present to the African psyche (Plate 31). The wood used is from a hard-wood tree, usually *dondol* (*Bombax cornui*).

The geometric style is also reflected in the ancestor images, and in those designed to stimulate fertility, such as are given to young girls at puberty. We also find statues of twins. The masks are mostly zoomorphic and are often reproductions of the totem animal, the antelope. In more recent types, small decorative shells are used. The chief centres of activity are Bamako on the Niger, Furi-Buguni and Kinian. At Bamako there are exquisite examples of door-knobs, bolts, and doors, in which mechanical ingenuity inspires works of art rich in ornamental *motifs*. The Bambara sculptors belong to the caste of smiths, at one time shunned and despised for reasons explained at the beginning of this chapter. The social structure of the Bambara rests on traditional agrarian institutions and hinges on the society for youths, called *Ntomo*, and for adults, called *Komo* and *Wara*.

But where such traditions have been preserved nearly intact has been among the Dogon or Habe, who live on the high table-land of the central Niger. It is a region difficult of access and defended by natural barriers. Here an ancient cosmogony, inherited from very remote times, provides the framework for tribal institutions. The artists are thus in possession of an elaborate symbology which they can use for sculptural and decorative purposes. The original hermaphroditic element is perceptible in the statuettes and ritual instruments used by the Hogon, or high priests. Maternity statues with the woman's head carved in the shape of a vulture (Plate 32) are characteristic of this group. The same distinctive form is found in the Nimba statuary of Guinea.

The cosmological cult aims at the identification of pulsations or cosmic cycles to which individuals adapt themselves by reflecting in their activities the hierarchy of the forces of nature. Ancestor worship is deeply ingrained, and inspires the hieratic images of the two principal centres of this region, Hombori and Duenza. There is a hieratic flavour about the images of two seated people, a position which is invariably related to an archaic prototype.

The legacy of an early cultural cycle is perpetuated on the walls of caves used for preserving ceremonial masks. It is possible that these caves were also used for initiation rites. The pictures are polychrome, executed in red, white and black ochre. They show a tendency towards abstraction, and reproduce masked dancers, spirits and animals, as well as cult instruments. The masks are zoomorphic, representing the totem animal of the clan. They are primarily used in the associations for youths, called *Nama*, whose members are individually responsible for making their own masks. Like the Bambara, the Dogon also produce elaborately carved doors and bolts in which the human figure often appears in stylised form.

The Mossi do not appear to be particularly outstanding in any respect, apart from a pronounced pugnacity which impels them to absorb neighbouring peoples older than themselves. Among these are the Fulse who belong to the same archaic cycle as the Dogon. The Fulse have retained the most interesting traditions in their *Wango* society, an assembly of young masked dancers. A rite connected with the ancient Fulse traditions prescribes that the masks used annually in the *Wango* should mount guard over a certain sacred tree. The fruit of this tree is known as *m'peku*, and it is taboo to gather *m'peku* before it is fully ripe. These masks also reproduce totem animals in stylised form. Among these is the antelope, which appears decorated with polychrome geometric patterns. It is interesting to note that an ancestor image, such as one finds among the Bobo, has been incorporated in this mask. With the Bobo, masked dances serve to establish communion with the ancestral spirits.

The region inhabited by the Bobo occupies not only a part of the Sudan but, as with the Senufo, extends as far as the Ivory Coast. Their conditions of life are primitive and their art products—with stylistic centres at Bobo Diulasso and at Bobo Ule—are related to those of the Dogon. Apart from the masks with customary totemic *motifs*, the bronze objects produced by *cire perdue* are worth mentioning; they consist of bracelets, ear-rings, pendants, etc. Lem, who recognised the spiritual influence of Benin productions, admits the possibility of their having learned the technical process of smelting from Benin. Amulets, equestrian statuettes, and images of twins were all produced by means of smelting.

In the wooden statues the trunk is elongated and cylindrical. It rests on the lower members while the arms hang in parallel lines from the shoulders to the pelvis. There is a resemblance here to the statue oracle called Yodola, whose response was delivered by the sound of a bell shaken in front of it. Unlike the Mossi, the Senufo or Senofo are a peaceful people. They are composed of small farmers who were once forced to fortify their villages against predatory slave traders. Extending as far as the Ivory Coast, the 800,000 members of this tribe are subdivided into twenty-five groups, each with its different language and customs.

The association that retains political power and whose authority runs in each village is that of the *Do*, which means 'secret'. The totem animal is the bird Kono, sometimes reproduced on the *Do* masks. These are naturally zoomorphic, with a characteristic gash for the mouth, and very large teeth, tusks and horns. However, many examples, some of which are of a high standard artistically, lack these attributes (Plate 33). The bird Kono also appears in the statues, giving a singular form to the women's head-dresses (Plate 35). The images of these birds were used in a sacred dance called *kurbi*, corresponding to that of the antelope among the Bambara. Two Kono in wood, representing a male and a female, were placed on perches which the dancers held in their hands while they imitated the flight of the bird. The chief stylistic centre is Korhogo, whence come also the so-called 'Janus masks' flanked and surmounted by the symbol of the Kono, used in the *Do* dance (Plate 34).

As among the neighbouring peoples, such as the Senufo, statuettes abound to promote young girls' fertility, the double images of twins, besides cosmetic boxes for unguents, etc.

The Malinke, like the Mandingue, are of scant artistic importance; they inhabit parts of French Guinea. Islamic influence has taken the link with the old ways. What remains now is the result of the influence of neighbouring peoples, such as the Senufo. The fertility statuettes called *numumoni*, 'the small people of the smiths', are an example of this. Both the statues and masks are decorated with little shells.

Guinea, whether Portuguese or French, is the seat of a social order based on a matriarchy, and the name itself, in the Baga language, means 'woman'. Here too the influence of Islam has almost totally eradicated the ancient beliefs, and very little of the artistic traditions has survived. Kjersmeier, however, reproduces a bird called Foho. It is used as an upper part of the mask in the dances of the secret society, *Simo*. The masks and statues called *Nimba* are designed to protect mothers. They are characterised by a hooked nose and a vulture-shaped skull. There is a correspondence between this *motif* and the same bird in the Egyptian ideogram, *mutt*, which means 'mother'.

In the region of the Kissi of Guinea, stone statuettes have been discovered called *pombo*, or 'images of the dead' that can be connected with the *numori* of the Mendi, examined in the preceding chapter. They are distinguished from them, however, by the lack of any distinctive characteristics, such as the treatment of the eyes, or the torso, which in the case of the *pombo* is a cylindrical shape.

The present wooden sculptures of the Mendi have nothing in common with the archaic *numumoni* images, which were almost certainly produced by a totally different race who in a remote era occupied this region of Sierra Leone. In rare cases, the artist is inspired by steatite models; but for the most part the images of the Mendi are distinguished by their extraordinarily long necks which are decorated with necklaces. These elongated wooden statues with their small, graceful, finely worked heads look not unlike rather elegant skittles (Plate 36). They are mostly female images and were used as oracles in a secret society for women, called the *Yassi*. The pythoness, Ya-mama, would fall into a magically induced lethargy which was followed by a dance. In the course of the dance the responses were made by the movements of the statuettes, *minsereh*, held in her hand. The smooth, polished appearance of these images is due to the frequent greasings that form part of the magic ritual.

Another female secret society that superintends the initiation of young girls is the *Bundu*, or *Sande*. The geometrical incisions executed on the cylindrical surface of the masks of this society animate the whole with a vibrant play of light.

The predominant male society is the powerful *Poro*. It is particularly influential in Liberia, as well as in Guinea. In the *Poro* the mask is regarded as the seat of a spirit, its value residing in the object itself and not in any transforming faculty on the part of the person wearing it. Among the numerous stylistic variations is an elongated beak used in initiation ceremonies. Some masks are similar to those of the Dan on the Ivory Coast. They have tubular eyes and their tusks and horns are rhythmically balanced one against the other.

Among the Dan, or Yakoba of the Ivory Coast, there are numerous varieties of mask: from the naturalistic negroid type, the style termed Guere-Urobe (Plate C), to the more stylised sort, or to those shaped like a beak, found in the southern regions such as Liberia. The Dan, composed of about a 100,000 members, are gathered chiefly in the Man district. They produce anthropomorphic heads furnished at the top with a lock of ritual feathers, a fashion that recalls the terracottas of Sao. The Guro consist of about 100,000 persons who live in the region of Zuenula. They are distinguished by an extremely sophisticated type of human mask, used in the dances of the secret societies *Gore* and *Guie*. The face is elongated with a large, slightly convex forehead. The nose is finely shaped and the eyes slightly pointed. A bird or a lock of hair falls over the forehead which, in some specimens of particular beauty, is surmounted by a horn (Plate B). There are no statuettes from this tribe but only anthropocephallic shuttles.

Among the peoples of the Ivory Coast, the Baule have produced work that is not only of ethnographic interest but also of high artistic value. But apart from their intrinsic qualities, the objects are also distinguished by the ends for which they were intended. They were not solely ritualistic or magical, but aesthetic: they were made to embellish and lighten the walls of the living, as well as those of the dead, by means of their beauty.

Women loved to have their portraits sculpted by famous artists (Plates 37, 38), and whoever set out on a long journey left an image of himself with his family, so that they would remember him. An ornamental *motif* skilfully exploited by the sculptors is provided by the tattoo marks executed in relief. They cover the body, starting from the face, and make a rich and indeed personal addition to many of the models.

The hair is reproduced with great care. The artist toyed with various elaborate *coiffures* in the manner of Parisian hairdressers. We find beehives such as are obtained by backcombing, intricately knotted hair, and plaits. The figurines of the elders have all the qualities of exquisite finish and composition that characterise Baule statuary (Plate 39). Their function corresponds to that of the Egyptian *Ka* images, which are placed in the tomb as a point of attraction towards which the spirit of the deceased is intended to be drawn.

Elegance, sober refinement, absolute technical control, attention paid to the final polishing and greasing—all these are the qualities that strike us in Baule statuary. The same traits are to be found in the masks, which range from singularly sophisticated reproductions of the human face (Plate 40), to anthropomorphic representations of specific animals such as the interesting mask that reproduces an elephant-man (Plate 41). We are reminded of the South African rock pictures in Natal, among which we find a zoomorphic creature of this type, with the body of a man.

The high quality of Baule sculpture is shown in objects of everyday use, such as shuttles, spoons, musical instruments, etc., all decorated with a human head. Pendants in the form of human heads, or animals, were made by means of *cire perdue*, among which we find the stylised figure of a ram; and there are also bronze objects which were used to weigh gold-dust. But these productions are closely connected with Ashanti art of which they are the descendants. We shall deal with these minor productions in the next chapter.

Concentrating on Ashanti statuary we come across curious images called *Akua Ba* (Plate 42). These were used by pregnant women. If a woman wanted a boy the statue was round-faced, stylised, with protuberant features. If she wanted a girl, the head was square and topped by a lock of hair. The influence of the statue thus manifested itself through, and by means of, its actual geometrical form. The same system as is found in the *Akua Ba*, of depicting the features in relief, is also met with in terracotta heads used for funerary purposes.

The kingdom of the Ashanti, who at present number a million people, makes its first historical appearance towards the end of the seventeenth century as a theocratic state in which the king held both sacred and profane powers. He also held the monopoly of gold, and the goldsmiths belonged to the hereditary nobility. The council of elders, which constituted a species of senate, ratified the laws drawn up by the king, whose despotic power was thus limited. The kingdom of the Ashanti lasted until 1895, when it became a British protectorate. The opulence of this kingdom is reflected in the pieces designed for the court, in its jewellery and in domestic objects. Its general aesthetic character is one of sobriety, while its ritual statues in their later forms are stylised. Among the cult objects worth mentioning is

99

a talking drum, caled *ntumpane*, a word that strangely recalls τυριπανον or 'tympanum', the drum sacred to Cybele in classical antiquity.

The art of Dahomey has been dealt with in the preceding chapter. Here we can note the connection between it and an equestrian statuette which commonly represents the sky god Obatala, an important iconographic element in Yoruba mythology. The civilisation of this ancient people has spread outward from cultural centres in the same way as did the art of the sacred city of Ife. Its influence on neighbouring civilisations was direct and profound. The myths of a people's origins often repay study, for at the very least one can usually deduce from them certain historical relationships. We have studied the myth of the sea-god Olokun in connection with the history of Benin. Yoruba mythology, perpetuated in the iconography of the epoch immediately following their presumed foundation, will similarly help us to a better understanding of their origins. There is an important study by Sergy on this subject.

Legend attributes the foundation of the Yoruba state to Shango, a mythical hero deified as the god of thunder and lightning, who was the object of the most important Yoruba cult. In common with other African peoples, the Yoruba did not make the Supreme God, Olorun, an object of devotion. He was considered a being too exalted and remote for that: he was thought of as absolutely indifferent to the creation that continually proceeded from him. Their religious attentions were, on the contrary, directed to intermediaries between the Absolute and our world, the Orisha—that is, the divinities and demi-gods, spirits and personifications of the forces of nature. The most important among the Orisha, Obatala, was charged by Olorun with giving the finishing touches to the created world and to man. The son born to Obatala from his union with the goddess Odudua was called Aganju, who in his turn married a divinity, Yemaja. As the myth proceeds through its later geneological phases there are marked correspondences with

PLATE D. Wooden polychrome mask of the Ijaw. Height 2 ft. 2 ins.
S. Nigeria.

the Oedipus cycle. Indeed, Yemaja's son, Orugan, first king
of the Yoruba, developed a morbid passion for his mother
and married her. The goddess, overwhelmed by horror,
fled, but in her flight she stumbled and fell to the ground,
thus giving birth to a series of Orishas, of which the first
was Shango, followed by three sisters (who in their turn
became his wives), besides other brothers who became
patrons of various human activities and of the processes
found in nature. Shango became king of the ancient Oyo
(Eyeo or Katunga), asserting himself by means of his
despotic character and his natural endowments as a warrior,
for he was a leader of indomitable courage, capable of
breathing fire through his mouth. He was deposed and
forced to flee, together with his wives, of whom, however,
only one, Oya, remained faithful to him to the end.
Shango finally committed suicide by hanging himself from
a tree, called *ayan*, which after his death was considered
sacred and used for carving cult objects associated with
his rite.

His reign had lasted for seven years. It was therefore
established that Yoruba kings could reign for seven years
and no longer. Many legends arose round the death of
Shango, not all of them remarkable for their consistency.
One of these tells how his people, in search of his body,
having reached the holy tree, found there only a pit from
the end of which an iron chain could be seen emerging,
while there came a far-off sound of voices. In this place,
called Kuso, they established the centre of his cult where
his priests, each with twelve acolytes, presided. Another
legend tells how Shango climbed to heaven by means of
the iron chain. There he dwells in his palace among the
clouds hurling his red-hot iron chain (lightning) against his
enemies. He had been particularly attached to his horses
in his life, and it was said that he took many of them
with him to his celestial seat. In his iconography he
almost invariably appears on horseback. Archaeological
research has sought to disentangle the historical elements
in the Shango legend from the purely mythical ones. As

Frobenius tells us, the ancient Oyo excavations have brought to light clay columns covered with carved wooden panels with plaques of copper and of beaten bronze that are of great beauty. One cannot help wondering whether these are the originals of the corresponding Benin plaques which used to decorate the Oba's palace.

Frobenius also holds that the Shango legend may have had its historical origins in the north, at Nupe. L. J. Moire, in his history of Nubia (in which, however, he makes no mention of the Yoruba) records the Meroitic legend in which the founder of Nubia is described as being the god Shango. And it is singular, from this point of view, that one of the titles attributed to him by the Yoruba is 'Oba-Kuso', that is 'King of Kuso'. In Nubia, the title of Shango was 'King of Kush'.

Another connection with Nubia is the possible identification of Shango with the bronze warrior found at Jebba, to which reference has already been made, and on whose helmet appears the image of a vulture, related to the Egyptian goddess Nekhebit. The studies of Meyerowitz have emphasised various Nubian elements found on this bronze.

Among the Yoruba, as among many other peoples, the stone relics of the neolithic epoch were regarded as thunderbolts: that is to say, they were thought to have been produced by strokes of lightning. For Shango was lord of the lightning, and one of his titles was Jakuta or 'thrower of stone'. Lucas believed this word to be of Egyptian origin. He gives it the meaning 'living soul of Ptah' (j-akhu-[p]-tah) and records how, among the Egyptians, the god Ptah was embodied in a single slab of stone. However, further philological and historical study are necessary before we can arrive at a firm opinion on this point.

As far as the horse is concerned, it is, as we have said, to be found in connection with every composition representing Shango. The Yoruba custom of sacrificing a chief's horse after his death is in accordance with the finds of the royal

The Sculpture. Part Two

tomb of Qostol, a region to the south of Abu Simbel. In this case, the king's horses which he used in battle were impaled on the staircase leading down to his tomb while, similarly, his slaves were put to death in order to provide him with a retinue in the next world. Among the Yoruba, the horses were slain on the actual superstructure of the tomb, while the ritual phrase was pronounced: 'The Alafin (chieftain) rides towards the kingdom of Shango.'

It is impossible, within the limits of this study, to examine all the points of contact between Nubia and Yoruba, which have anyway been admirably treated by Segy; but we cannot pass over one important iconographic element: 'the two-edged battle axe'.* This ritual instrument is a part of the Shango cult and is made of wood from the sacred tree. It is more or less stylised, and sometimes shown protruding from the head of the goddess Oja, faithful consort of Shango (Plate 43). In many cases, the goddess herself, 'the Lady of the axe', holds this instrument in her hand which, besides being used in her cult ceremonies, was also placed in the fields to protect crops. At other times, it served as a primitive lightning conductor, deflecting the fiery javelins of the god Shango. It is to be presumed that this double axe, perpetuated for us in the wooden iconography, may originally have had blades of neolithic flint.

It is worth noting that there is evidence of the use of the double axe in ancient Egypt up to the time of the first dynasty; while in the fifth dynasty we find the title, 'Priest of the double axe'. In addition, the 'Palermo fragment' shows a double axe held by a Pharaoh of the old kingdom. As a cult instrument, the double axe is found in an extremely wide area of the Mediterranean, from Sardinia to the regions of Mycenaean-Cretan culture. Archaeological

* The double axe is called Oshe and is used in the ritual of Shango when the priest is in a state of possession. For further reference see 'The Symbolism and Ritual Context of the Yoruba Laba Shango', by Joan Wescott and Peter Morton-Williams. Journ. R.A.I. Vol. 92, Pt. I, 1962.

finds have brought to light very old altars surmounted by this symbol. It would thus be extremely interesting to learn of its presence as a cult object among different civilisations is due to the civilisation superimposing itself on another, or whether one is dealing simply with a recurrent vision of the same sacred reality, objectivised in the same way by various civilisations who have in fact had no physical contact with each other.

The method of comparative statistics, of which Frobenius was such a devout adherent, would provide a suitable line of approach for research in this field. This being so, it might be as well to outline the fundamentals of the method in the words of its creator. The most confused and often contradictory ideas have gathered around the name of Frobenius, and of his work; and this confusion makes itself felt even among Africologists. It is certainly true that many of his ideas are highly personal and controversial. They can, and do, excite lively discussion. But it is to Frobenius's lasting credit that he was the first to bring into focus the essential elements of African civilisations, stimulating a renewed interest in their comparative study.

The relative attitudes of Frobenius, Ankermann and Gräbner to the 'applied method' are contained in *Zeitschrift für Ethnologie,* 1905. Here is a selection of some of the more significant passages in which Frobenius explains his position:

. . . This method concerns me personally because it was born of the works which I have cited here. I must confess that, in part, these works to-day fail to satisfy me. When, after the publication of a genuine work, one sees that it contains several errors, the best thing is to find the courage to say: *Pater peccavi.* And it is the more fitting that I should do this since among those who reviewed my works when they appeared I have not found one who recognised my errors, and I am convinced that if I continue to maintain silence these errors will never be put right.

The Sculpture. Part Two

The statistical part of the method is based as follows: in a given part of the earth I find an element, and then I make a corresponding find, and then another. The individual elements are compared and found to have the same form. In another part of the earth I find the same or similar forms, with the same dimensions. Then various geographic areas are explored, and one can be sure that the majority of the areas investigated will yield the same form. But to the question whether the similarity of these forms derives from a common parentage, the statistical part of the method cannot provide an answer. One cannot in this case proceed as when one is examining the diffusion of a race of monkeys. This is to discover a complete vital existence, while a bow that we find somewhere, or an arrow or a hut, are only a fragment of a vital organism. We ought therefore to try to produce groups of the same dimensions that may be linked internally in a living and organic fashion. . . .

The most important question is this: is it possible to produce biological proofs for the organic connection of modes of culture and their development? I maintain that these proofs exist, but if we wish to find them we must make some change in the method used until now. We ought not to content ourselves with saying: Here we have this form of shield and here the other form, but we ought instead to look for the forms of development and evolution of shields. I believe that this second part of my method, the method of the history of developments, is the most important. Thus, for example, round huts can be identical from the outside in various parts of the earth. But before positing an organic link we ought to know the internal structure, the construction, the change of construction according to the dimensions. I believe one must above all pay attention to this biological side of the method. For the rest, by following strictly statistical methods, I have reached conclusions that are too general. Only by magnanimously and indulgently disregarding the small errors inevitable in the statistical analyses of the history of developments can we hope to be able to arrive at wider conclusions.

Ankermann's reply equally deserves our attention:

> Frobenius is perfectly right when he emphasises the necessity to limit oneself to observing the surface appearances of objects, and says that, to use his example, one cannot classify as 'round huts' all circular constructions, but that it is necessary also to look at the principle of construction. That I likewise have followed this method is shown from the fact that I have termed the huts of the Masai, and of the Somali, 'bee-hive' huts, inasmuch as they have not got a circular plan. Apart from this obvious objection I do not know what one could say against this method nor do I see what other way besides that followed by Frobenius and by us, can be followed.

If I have digressed in this exposition of Leo Frobenius's method, it is because its application, from half a century ago until to-day, has produced results of first importance in the field of the comparative history of civilisations and particularly of those of Africa. Moreover, it may well be helpful to the reader to know what Frobenius himself had to say about his method, more particularly as the passage in question is not easily accessible to everyone.

Returning to the sculpture of the Yoruba, we note how the tribal markings are sometimes perpetuated on the mask. In this instance, they are represented by a triple scarification, such as we have already observed on the Esie statues, held to be the claw mark of the totemic leopard, Agassu. Clay images, their heads decorated with feathers, are also found among the southern Yoruba. Their use, as we have seen, is common to various tribes and could derive from a parent concept diffused over a wide area.

We also find statuettes of couples depicting twins, the *ibeij*, which we mentioned earlier and which probably

The Sculpture. Part Two

originate from the same area. The ritual instruments called *edan* are equally found in pairs. They were used by the *Ogboni* society, one of the most powerful in West Africa. These *edan* consist of two bars of iron, on which two human figures, one of either sex, joined by means of a chain through the head, have been cast in bronze or, more accurately, in brass. Sometimes these images are cast in a single bar which they serve to decorate at either end (Plate 44). Their exact purpose is unknown.

Oracle tables, either circular or rectangular, were also important. The wood was carved round the edges, while the space where the dice or sand was thrown was left free. The position in which the dice or sand fell in relation to the surrounding carved figures was the clue to the diviner's 'interpretation'. The image of the god Edschu was enthroned in the middle. Yoruba art, whether in the archaic forms of Ife and, indirectly, of Benin, or in its later, more linear sculpture, is indispensable for an understanding of the African soul.

The Ibibio of Nigeria, constituting a group of 750,000 people, differ from other tribes in the type of their wooden sculpture. The constituent elements are unusual in that they are worked separately and not articulated as part of a single block. The masks present a wide variety of models —from the abstract, with polychrome effects, to the naturalistic. The Ijaw tribe use masks whose circular surface seems to be cut across by a wide arrow. The eyes, the nose and the mouth protrude and assume the geometrical forms of cylinders, rhombi, etc. (Plate D). Witchcraft is particularly widespread among this tribe who for this purpose use wax statues. The quality of Owo statuary probably reflects the proximity of the naturalistic centre of Benin. Rams' heads provide a common *motif*, as do anthropocephalic sculptures ornamented with rams' horns.

The people of the Cameroons, particularly the Ekoi, are distinguished by the way they use the hide of a particular animal, tanned and skilfully stretched to cover the heads of the wearers, as well as the masks themselves. Originally this covering was of human skin; later the skins of animals were substituted, among them that of the antelope. These pieces are singularly realistic, an effect which is increased by the use of human hair for forehead and beard. An Anjang piece, with an unusually Mongol cast of face, is interesting in this respect (Plate 45). The skin of the 'Janus masks' are often painted white for female faces and black for male. Both statues and masks have hard, cruel expressions, evocative of the more brutal natural forces.

The lesser groups in the Cameroons, Bamessing, Babungo, Bamilike, Bamun and Bali, use clay pipes whose bowls are worked in the shape of a human figure with a disproportionately large head. The Bekom have monumental masks and chairs decorated with zoomorphic *motifs*. One *motif* has two leopards like those of Benin, with a king between them. Such *motifs* are of special interest since the leopard was the Benin symbol for the king. There is also an interesting throne belonging to this tribe, which realistically depicts the king in a life-size image. The stool supporting the bucranium is joined to his knees (Plate 46). Copper bolts are set in the face, which is framed by a human head of hair, and the eyebrows are also 'natural'. The necklace and the sceptre have a polychrome appearance obtained by means of white and blue beads. The same Grassland region has produced a surprisingly realistic head of a woman carved in wood and with unmistakably negroid features. The eyes are of inlay-work and have a remote Egyptian look about them (Plate 47). There is also an important bronze piece (Plate 79) from this region, which we shall look at in the appropriate chapter.

The Duala do not appear to have made statues, but only masks, the more interesting of which are used by the secret society, *Ekongolo*. The style varies from the polychrome zoomorphic, to stylised representations of the human face. They have a strange head-dress which reproduces a vibrating, wave-like *motif*, and these head-dresses are also polychrome (Plate 48). A characteristic mask of this sort

56. Detail of a Bakota figure of painted wood. The statue itself is
1 ft. 8½ ins. in height. Congo.

57. Bakuba cup (rhyton) of painted wood. Height 8½ ins. Congo.

58. Bakuba wooden sculpture. Height 1 ft. 2 ins.
ex-Belgian Congo.

59. Top of a Baluba sceptre. The sceptre 3 ft. 5 ins. in height.

60. Baluba mask of painted wood. Height 1 ft. 4 ins.
ex-Belgian Congo.

61. Bapende wooden mask. Height 1 ft. ex-Belgian Congo.

62. Pendant mask in ivory. Height 2¼ ins. Bapende,
ex-Belgian Congo.

63. Bakaya wooden mask. The face is red with a smaller white mask. Height 1 ft. 6 ins. Width 1 ft. 10 ins. ex-Belgian Congo.

is produced by the Abu. The general silhouette is that of a horned animal. From the projecting ears it could be a buffalo. The distinctive element, however, is provided by a small crocodile shown clinging to the horns with its hind-paws, and to the forehead with its fore-paws. Its long snout extends down the front part of the face where the nose should be, reaching as far as the painted mouth (Plate 49). The effect is startling and, presumably, goes far beyond that required, namely, to stimulate excitement in a ritual dance.

Moving on to French Equatorial Africa, we find a tribe whose productions are extremely abstract. This is the Bakota, in Gabon. As with other peoples of Africa, the principal cult is that of ancestor worship. The skulls, heaped together in sacks or baskets, are guarded in holy huts outside the village enclosure. So far there is nothing exceptional. But on these baskets full of skulls the Bakota set special images as guardians (Plate 50). These images average 1 ft. 4 ins. in height, are made with wood ornamented with brass, and are practically all 'head'. The body, indeed, is reduced to a lozenge-shaped outline which is the same in every specimen, while the face is subject to numerous stylistic variations.

The features are either executed in full relief, or tend towards a stylised expression which, in some instances, results in complete abstraction. The ears are missing, but on the side of the head a species of halo frames the face, sometimes terminating in two small pendants. The top is crowned by a species of cocked hat, like a half-moon reversed. Taken as a whole these figures are extraordinarily evocative of other-worldly powers. The resolution of the interior mingling of lozenge and oval contributes to the exterior play of lines and surfaces which are thus arrested and brought to a standstill. The indigenous people called this figure *mbulu ngulu*, or 'image of the spirit of the dead'. It is not in itself a cult object, but the Bakota stand before it if they wish to ask one of their immediate forefathers for some special favour. They repeatedly clap their hands and at this sound the spirit of the dead enters the statue and listens to the petitions addressed to him.

The strangeness of these images, so far removed from any other sculpture, has aroused the interest of scholars, who have proposed the most diverse and sometimes contradictory theories to account for them. Frobenius holds that they are masks, or, alternatively, ancestor images; von Sydov holds that they are symbolic representations of the human body; Segy concurs in this opinion, but goes further, for he believes that the lozenge *motif* expresses the idea of the disintegration of the human body after death. The half-moon shape which acts as a head-dress has also been the subject of various interpretations. For Frobenius, it is the equivalent of a solar nimbus, while von Sydow treats it as the crescent moon—the image itself serving simply to call the attention of the passer-by to the contents of the baskets.

Each of these theories is partly true, but none wholly so. We must remember how in Africa, death goes hand in hand with fear of the possible harmful effects of spirits on the living. In the course of this study we have already dwelt more than once on this point, and it would be tedious to repeat ideas already explained. Nevertheless it is worth emphasising that funeral stele, trees placed near tombs, and images of the dead, all serve the same purpose, that of 'laying' the spirit, the shade of the departed, or the *Ka*, and preventing any such manifestations of the deceased emerging from their tombs. The Bakota had the same conception. They evolved an image capable of 'absorbing' the spirit of the dead. For the rest, the name itself attributed to these images, 'images of the spirit of the dead', immediately establishes a correspondence with the statues of the *Ka*.

As for the lozenge that takes the place of the trunk and members, although accepting Segy's general idea of disintegration, it must be made clear that this disintegration referred to the wish to preclude movement, by depriving the statue of its lower limbs. The spirit was thus 'laid': it had to rest where the skull was left. To cancel or annul a part of the body in a representational image is a magical concept not peculiar to Africa; we find the same idea clearly expressed in ancient Egypt, where it was meant to effect a paralysing action, through the close connection between the model and the plastic representation.

As for the head-piece, I agree with von Sydow, that it is a species of lunar halo. We have already pointed out the influence this planet exercised on African conceptions, particularly in the context of apparitions and spectres. But in the case of the Bakota images, the idea has not been sufficiently developed. The comparison with specific pieces from the Cameroons suggests the possibility that the Bakota half-moon, or felucca, may at least initially have depicted a real object with which were connected ideas of dignity and command. In the Cameroons, a Banka throne shows the figure of a chieftain or conqueror, seated with a commanding air on a level surface like a small bench, which is supported on the back of a slave (Plate 51). The interesting point about this 'throne' is the felucca that the diminutive 'Napoleon' wears on his head. The small bench is circumscribed by a wave-like *motif*, symbolising water. It is thus possible that the image may have been intended to represent a chief come from the sea, an admiral of some fleet, or a conqueror come to impose his law. We are confronted with the idea of leadership in association with a particular head-piece. This image is also interesting because of the lozenge *motif*, which is reproduced on the body of the slave who supports the bench. Besides this object's comparative value in relation to the Bakota, the throne may well be regarded as an eloquent monument to a certain type of colonialism.

Preserved in Berlin, but originating from the Cameroons, there is an image of a major demon of the Bangu-Bangangte. It is ithyphallic with the body painted entirely in red (Plate 52), and is an interesting example of the transposition of the felucca from human to metaphysical iconography. In the first instance, one is dealing with the reproduction of a commander, that is, of a human being.

Here, on the contrary, we are in the 'spirit world', and the head-piece, in which ideas of power pre-exist, indicates the attributes of a major demon. In view of similar ideas found elsewhere, it would not be surprising if this form of iconography were developed among the Bakota as part of their funerary images. In the stylised felucca they found a means of indicating the dignified position usually accorded to the spirits of the departed.

Besides this, it seems likely that in the stages of this process, other specifically eschatological elements may have entered into the original conception. These would consist of such ideas as are normally connected with the lunar halo *et similia*. Moreover, apart from anything else, the actual shape of the head-piece, reminiscent of a reversed half-moon, would have evoked ideas of command and authority. It is worth recording that in the goldsmith work of the Ivory Coast there exists a sickle moon in reverse, very like the symbol of the Bakota, and called—predictably enough in the light of our thesis—*Saraï*, the moon.

Among the innumerable morphological varieties of the *mbulu ngulu* we find a common means of sex identification. The male images have convex faces, those of the women concave ones. In the case of young girls, the figure or image is generally modelled on a reduced scale.

The art of the Kuyu or Basochi is centred on the production of linear, anthropocephalic, polychrome batons used in the ritual dance *Kebe-Kebe*. These batons, however, are rarely of much artistic worth. An exception to this is found in the examples in the Charles Ratton Collection in Paris, one of which is reproduced here (Plate 53).

The art of the M'Pongwe of Ogué is inspired by the kingdom of the dead. The Ogué emigrated from the interior to the coastal regions. Two powerful female secret societies, the *Mukui* and the *Okuwe*, practise rites whose exact import is extremely obscure. The masks which are used in these rites constitute the characteristic art form of the M'Pongwe. Sculptured in wood and finely worked, they represent only female faces, and these are of outstanding beauty, even according to our Western taste. The face is oval and generally a little elongated. The periphery encloses plastic masses and is, in its turn, framed by a high, elaborate head-dress piled in one or more coils of hair that swell towards the crown and then fall down on either side. It is a mode calculated to exploit the chromatic contrasts of the mask in the most skilful manner. The head-dress is raven black and the face white, animated by scarifications executed geometrically in lozenges or squares of a reddish colour, while the lips are also red. The half-closed eyes are obtained by means of a narrow slit cut parallel to the arch of the eyebrows, accentuating the oriental character of the entire piece (Plate 54).

The startling realism of these masks, which admirably captures the celebrated beauty of the M'Pongwe women, is explained by the fact that they are real portraits. But since their purpose is magical their method of execution is magical also. The witch-sculptor selects his model from among the young girls of the tribe and works, unknown to her, on the mask of her face. He is constrained to pay her assiduous courtship, and under the cloak of caressing her face he 'steals' her features from her. He measures with his fingers the distances between eyes, ears, mouth, and their proportions; then he faithfully reproduces them from memory as soon as he is back in his *atelier*. The courtship lasts until the work, similar in every respect to the original, albeit a trifle stylised, is completed. The sculptor then proceeds to the last stage, the colouring. The face is painted white with kaolin, because this is the colour attributed to spectres and the mask is destined to serve the dead. The narrow eye-slits, responsible for the strangely oriental look, are the only features which do not reflect the actual appearance of the M'Pongwe women. They are a ritual requirement intended to prevent the spirit evoked during the dance from adversely affecting the wearer of the mask.

A study of vampirism, common to various peoples, explains the custom of 'lending' to the spirit of a dead person the features of a living one. The *rapport* established between the victim and his unknown assailant is one of identity. This identity is dynamised by ritual practices, culminating in a ceremonial dance allowing the spirit to enter into contact with the person represented by the mask. The spirit will absorb his, or in this case her, vitality in the manner of a vampire, exercising its function through a magnetic fluid. Not only this, but through the same channel, that is, the physical body of the unknowing victim, it relives all the sensations connected with physical pleasure.

A peculiarity of the dance in which such masks are used is that it takes place on stilts. In this way the dancers are, as it were, insulated from contact with the soil. Although various forms of vampirism are attested in the degenerate manifestations of African witchcraft, the case of the M'Pongwe is unique, as much from the fact that a portrait of the living serves the dead, as because of the sometimes exceptional artistic level attained by the masks. The M'Pongwe statues are of less importance than the masks, although they are unusual, as the eyes and tongue are worked in metal, generally copper.

The *bian* used by the Pangwe or Fang, who also come from Gabon, corresponds to the Bakota *mbulu ngulu*. The Pangwe or Fang, also known as the Pahuin, similarly place wooden images on top of sacks called *bieri*, which contain the skulls of their ancestors. In contradistinction to the productions of the Bakota, those of the Fang totally lack the abstract character of the *mbulu ngulu*. The Fang produced statuettes either of an entire figure, or of half a figure, or it may even be simply of a head resting on a long neck (Plate 55). The style of the face is concave; it is stylised; the eyes often look as though closed in sleep; the mouth is generally jutting forwards and sometimes seems to express melancholy. In some examples, as in the one reproduced, the face is surmounted by a head-dress that falls symmetrically on either side, and behind, the head. The fact that many of these images are no more than busts, or that they end without any indication of lower limbs, can again be related to the idea of keeping the spirit in one place or, as we should say, of 'laying' it. But while this is generally understood to be the case, it is not always so; for there is a certain type of small statue that reproduces the lower limbs in a special, slightly bent attitude. The arms are mostly folded across the breast, clasping some instrument, such as a sceptre, a baton, a cup, etc. The name of these images, *bian*, means 'medicine' or 'remedy', and could derive from the custom of placing them beside a sick person to aid his recovery. As among the Bakota, these images do not represent any single individual but, placed on the receptacle that contains the ancestral skulls, they make it possible for the required spirits to manifest themselves in turn by using them as their media. Besides this, the Fang keep the skulls of their grandparents in sacred huts inside their domestic enclosures. On these skulls, the Fang take the precaution of placing a funerary image, in order to lay the spirits of the dead. Sometimes wooden statuettes, decorated with metallic plaques, are painted white or black, according to the rite of the secret society for which they are designed.

Passing to the ex-Belgian Congo, the stylistic divisions traced by Olbrechts are as follows:

Southern Congo:
Bakongo, Babuende, Bateke, Bayaka, Bambala, Basuku, Bapende, Bambunda.

Bakuba:
Bashilile, Basongo-Meno, Dengese, Bakete.

Baluba:
Basonge, Balunda, Bena Kanioka, Batshioko, Wabembe.

Northern Congo:
Azande, Baboa, Bambole, Ngbandi, Ngbaka, Mangbetu, Wabembe, Warega.

This classification has a purely indicative value. Indeed, the number of tribes and, consequently, of styles and sub-styles is much higher in the Congo than elsewhere, but at least some of their characteristics must be enumerated.

The Azande, known also as the Niam-Niam, were famous for their multiple-bladed knife, the *shongo*, that they threw at the legs of their enemies, in the same way as the Bakuba. The extreme functionality of this weapon forced its creators to study the play of the blades in flight. They were counterbalanced in such a way that, rotating, they would inflict the maximum of harm. For this reason the *shongo* is of interest artistically as well as ethnographically. The Bahuana, besides producing statues of mother and child, are distinguished by a special ivory amulet worn round the neck as a pendant and showing a close analogy with the *Hei-Tiki* of New Zealand.

In the Congo, wooden sculpture found one of its greatest expressions among the Bakongo, the inhabitants *par excellence* of this region, as their name, 'People of the Congo', shows. The maternity statues are a characteristic product of this tribe. The mother's face is treated with particular care, down to the minutest detail, including teeth. In general, the head is out of proportion to the rest of the body and particularly to the lower limbs. But the rather elongated trunk does not render this imbalance at all unpleasant; on the contrary, a sense of dignity and pride pervades these statues (Plate E). Until recently, they were ascribed to a hypothetical tribe, the Mayombe, but the latest studies have demonstrated the non-existence of any such tribe, the name merely designating a region.

The technique of hollowing the mouth and eyes is exemplified in the face of a polychrome statue of singularly emotive intensity. It resembles 'Pierrot' in the act of performing his melancholy serenade (Plate 56). The Bakongo produced steatite statues whose attitudes are unique in African sculpture: the head is inclined to one side, or else the cheek rests on the palm of the hand.

The Bakuba or Bushongo, who, as we saw, owe their name to their type of throwing-knife, claimed that their kings were of divine origin. One of their sovereigns in the

PLATE E. 'Motherhood'. Bakongo statuette in wood, with brass ornamentation. Height 10 ins. ex-Belgian Congo.

seventeenth century, Shamba Balongongo, introduced the custom of ordering royal statues to perpetuate *ad infinitum* his own effigy and the effigies of his successors. Seventeen of these statues are still in existence, of which twelve have been identified or, more exactly, are known each to correspond to one of twelve named kings. True identification is peculiarly difficult, as they all conform to the standard model of the original statue of King Shamba. The execution is good and the images effectively communicate the sense of command and dignity that we encounter in the statuary of the Bakongo. A ritual drum, one of the royal attributes, is generally shown in front of the sovereign. At other times he is depicted grasping an elaborate knife called *Ikula*, while his neck is hung with necklaces which have been added separately—another point in common with Bakongo art.

While the art of royal portraiture was confined to one invariable form, the artist's fantasy found opportunities for self-expression in carving other objects of wood. Among these, the most notable are the ceremonial cups. They may take the form of a human head, or of a full-length figure, or may be shaped cylindrically and ornamented with geometrical *motifs*. There is a very wide range of these African *rhyton*, some of which are true masterpieces (Plate 57). The sometimes sophisticated expressions of the figures portrayed, the mastery of the chisel, whether displayed in the carving of large smooth surfaces or of minutely worked detail, together with the surface patina, all contribute to make these cups among the most characteristic expressions of Negro art. Some specimens are two-headed, the heads being joined internally and meeting in a single neck; others are shaped like a drum, in which case the handle is either decorated with anthropocephalic *motifs*, or else with a hand. One of the uses of these cups may have been to enact 'trial by ordeal'. When a crime had been committed, suspected persons were made to drink a poisonous potion from them. Death was regarded as at once evidence of guilt, and a fitting punishment.

An isolated example of the hand *motif* used as a handle

is to be found in a ritual instrument of the *Yolo* secret society. It consists of a curved left hand, and probably refers to the ancient custom by which admittance into the society was conditional on having cut off the left hand of an enemy. The geometric *motif* decorating the instrument (in common with decorative elements found on other objects) is part of a complex and elaborate symbology to which the Bakuba ascribe magic powers.

Yet another category of wooden sculptures is provided by cosmetic boxes, in which various unguents were kept, together with the red powder, called *tukula*, that the Bakuba rubbed on their bodies. Sometimes these boxes are shaped like a human face, slightly resembling the faces of the royal statues, although those on the boxes are notably more stylised. The mouth is in the form of two enclosed lozenges, one inside the other; while the scarifications running from the inside corner of the eye diverge, emphasising the Bakuba artists' predilection for geometric design.

Another type of receptacle, intended for the same purpose, was carved in the shape of a human figure. The effect is generally grotesque, the form being either that of a manikin standing upright, or else—and this suggests a protection against sleeping-sickness—of a creature with an enormous head on a very small insect body (Plate 58). The arms are depicted in a particularly interesting way. They emerge directly from the crouching shoulders, while the hands, on which rests the immoderately large head, are like all Bakuba work, treated with detailed care. The lozenge mouth, and the almond-shaped eyes, turn inwards in the distinctive stylistic expression peculiar to this tribe.

The masks represent a great variety of models, some of which skilfully exploit decorative polychrome *motifs* with small pearls and shells made to adhere to a support of cloth and hide. The mask called *mashaboy*, whose origin is ascribed to the seventy-third sovereign, Bo Kena, was worn by the chiefs and other dignitaries in memory of one of the clan heroes. Other specimens in wood bear the characteristics of Bakuba wooden sculpture, and are therefore easily recognisable. More difficult to identify are those painted in geometrical polychrome *motifs*. Finally, there is a special divining instrument called *itombwa*, which is in the form of an animal with an elongated body, something like a basset-hound. The figure is sometimes anthropocephallic.

The art of the Baluba, the ancient followers of the mythical chieftain Luba, comes from the regions of the south-eastern Congo. It represents the finest art work in the area. The female fertility images are of particular interest. They are shown in the classic position, with the hands supporting the breasts, typical of mother-iconography in archaic times. These statues are found either in isolation or as integrated elements in the royal sceptre. Their severe and meditative expressions and their strongly delineated features, express the sacredness of fertility (Plate 59). There is a disproportion between the lower limbs and the trunk and head, which last is invariably emphasised. The figures have decorative, geometric scarifications. They are also draped with necklaces of multi-coloured pearls, which are added separately to the statue.

Another typical Baluba statue—a common one in African statuary—is that of a kneeling woman, holding a circular vessel in her hands. The figure was designed as a protection for mothers, and may also have been used as a divining instrument. The image of an ancestor was placed in the vessel, which was shaken by an official. The auspices for the future child were interpreted according to the various positions that the image assumed. The child's name was also chosen by this technique, the inspiration being attributed to the spirit of one of the child's ancestors, who chose this way of maintaining the ancestral bonds. The same vessel, called *Kabila Ka Vilie*, 'the wife or daughter of the spirit', was used to hold the kaolin with which the witch-doctor smeared his body; while another term, *Kabila Ka Iulombo*, 'the beggar', refers to the custom of alms-gathering when one's wife is pregnant.

The Buli region has produced artistic work of particular beauty, among which is the fertility statue already examined, besides chairs supported by human figures. All the pieces share a profound and concentrated expression of face, partly due to the supple, sometimes angular, lips. The eyes, almost almond-shaped, lend a distinctly oriental air; the surface finish is dark and shining.

In Baluba statuary we must distinguish two fundamental types: the ancestor images, called *Mikisi Mihasi,* and those designed for magical practices, which were called *Mikisi Mihake.* The former, also known as *Bimnveleko* (that is, the 'resemblance') are equivalent to the Egyptian statues of the *Ka.* Their use to lay spirits of the dead is evident from the fact that they lack the lower limbs, thus recalling the idea of a stele. In spite of this, however, the face is treated realistically, whence the name 'resemblance'. This element constitutes another point of contact with the statues of the *Ka.* These images are distinguished from the magical *Mikisi Mihake* by a scrupulous attention to detail in the chiselling of the head-dress, and by the smoothness of the surface finish. The *Mikisi Mihake* are cruder; it is not really permissible to speak of them in artistic terms: their interest is in fact solely ethnographic. Shells, pearls, mirrors and little lumps of reputedly magical substances are added by the witch-doctor to the wooden statue, as occasion demands. A Baluba legend refers the origin of these images to Nkulu, the supreme spirit who lives in the depths of the sea. Nkulu allowed the sorcerer Bwana Kilumba to make a copy of the prototype in his possession, in order to lighten mankind's sufferings.

The Baluba also have a characteristic wooden head-rest. It sometimes depicts an embracing couple whose heads support the board for the sleeper's head. Apart from those having specific *motif*, constituting the support, this type of wooden head-rest is common in various African tribes. It was used in the earliest periods known to us, as well as in ancient Egypt.

Among the sceptres and batons, of which various

examples exist, there is an axe whose blade emerges like a tongue from a decorative head carved on the top of the haft. Various authors have assumed a wooden pole with an anthropocephalic *motif* to be a sceptre. Three wooden rods protrude from the head, the two at the side being inclined slightly forwards. Far from this being a symbol of kingship, these objects were in fact used as quivers.

Among the most interesting of all the Baluba masks are those which were used in the dance *makaye a Kifwebe* by the homonymous secret society. Here a dramatic tension is obtained by means of the opposition of geometric elements: a circular or spherical circumference, square and protuberant mouth, curved lines opposed to vertical or horizontal ones. Curves, angles, ellipses and squares, emphasised in the 'picture' of the mask, cast a vibrating effect over the whole, zebra-like design. The piece is brought startlingly alive, quite independently of its use in the dance (Plate 60).

Some specimens are unusually large, and some represent the so-called 'Janus', or duplex head. Quite different, on the other hand, are naturalistic masks of the human face furnished with horns, whose style links them to the productions of the Buli region. Ivory is used in amulets, and in an oracular instrument called *katatora*, which takes the form of a cylinder, topped by a human head.

The Bapende, who number about 25,000 people, inhabit the region of Léopoldville. Their art is above all noted for a very personal type of mask, called the *minyaki*, used in ritual dances and circumcision ceremonies. If in other regions it is the oval that predominates, the basis of these masks is unrelievedly triangular, both as regards the face and the individual features. The eyes are a protruding lozenge shape; the arch of the eyebrows is angled; the nose is represented by a point. An extremely sophisticated air, accentuated by the shape of the mouth, and by the half-closed eyelids, pervades the whole face (Plate 61).

Side by side with this characteristic type there coexist other masks either in wood, or in raffia and feathers. Their interest, at least on the artistic level, is more limited. Reproductions of masks in miniature are used as amulets and initiation badges. They preserve the sophisticated character of the larger masks, while some examples in ivory achieve a surprising degree of emotional intensity (Plate 62).

The productions of the Bayaka, or 'strong people', also have stylistic traits which make identification comparatively straightforward. The human nose is reproduced as a diminutive proboscis raised towards the sky. Sometimes it is bent backwards so that it touches the forehead. This feature is constantly found in the statues, masks and decorative *motifs* of daily objects. Lavachery compares this proboscis-nose to the nose of the god Chac in the Maya temple in Yucatan, although he hastens to emphasise that the resemblance can be nothing more than a curious coincidence.

The masks are generally polychrome. One of the principal types is called *nkisi*. It is characterised by half-open lips showing the teeth, and by a complicated hair-style. A smaller mask, round or square, indicates sex differentiation (Plate 63). Sometimes these masks have a pagoda-shaped headpiece, a *motif* also found on small domestic articles such as combs or hat-pins.

Bayaka statuary is rather coarse and sensual. In some of their pieces, when they wish to depict a woman's breasts cupped in her hands, they employ the curious device of carving the breasts on the sides of the arms. The ancient population of Angola carved their female statues in the same way, and it is presumably from them that this stylistic mannerism is derived (Plate 70).

The Bena Lulupa of the province of Lusambo have produced wooden statues of archaic excellence, unique of their kind. The elaborate tattoo marks in relief partially recall New Zealand work. The Bena Lulua statues, however, are crowned by a cone-shaped head-piece that remind one of the strange pyramidal patterns that the sea sometimes makes on sand. This statuary is chiefly remarkable for the unusually protuberant navel (Plate 64). Ancestor images, and images of mother and child, are wide-spread. Some statuettes show a seated man who props the weight of his head, which is outsize, on his two small arms. The fine tribal tattoo marks are repeated in the elaborate polychrome masks.

The Mangbetu of Stanleyville, who inhabit a region bordering on the former Anglo-Egyptian Sudan, express this proximity in their art products. In particular, the markedly dolichocephalic skull of their anthropomorphic images recall certain Egyptian sculptures. But this is not a case of simple deformation. The Mangbetu contract their children's heads with cords in early infancy, and their statuary faithfully reflects this custom. Among Mangbetu pieces there is a particular clay drinking vessel surmounted by a human head with an elaborate hair-style, which is reproduced in Plate 65.

From the Manyema region, between Lualaba and Tanganyika, comes an interesting wooden bench depicting a woman with both arms raised, holding a plate placed on her head (Plate 66). The piece is an example of an overtly geometric style. The lines of the chin, the breasts and the bent knees are all parallel. The nose is somewhat triangular, as is the face itself, and also the umbilical scarification. Until recently it was believed that Manyema was the name of a tribe. It is in fact the name of a district.

Among the various Congolese tribes the Warega are particularly celebrated for their ivory work. The name Warega is still generally used, although Balega has comparatively recently been found to be the true name of the tribe and Lega that of its members. A complex secret association, the *Bwami*, directed the tribe's social, political and religious life until 1948, the year in which it was abolished by the Belgian authorities under the pretext of criminal actions. The initiation ceremonies took place in a sacred hut in the centre of the village. These ceremonies effected the transmission of certain powers related to different ranks of society. The media by which the transmission of these powers was effected were ivory and wooden images whose possession was always a closely guarded secret.

These images consisted of wooden and ivory masks and of ivory statuettes. The ivory masks (Plate F) were used only by the highest grades in the society, and the ritual dances and songs accompanying their use emphasised the deference due to seniority and the distrust of new initiates. The wooden masks were called *kalagama*, that is, 'guardian' and were used both in initiation ceremonies and as a domestic protection for the members of the sect, who hung them up on the walls of their houses. There were eleven grades in the society, and only from the seventh upwards could the initiates possess a *kalagama*. This was generally furnished with a beard of vegetable fibre by which, during the ceremonies, it was held in the hand when it was not being worn. Some of the wooden masks tend to be abstract, and all of them are larger than those in ivory (Plate 68). Proverbs, or maxims, are connected with these masks, as with the statues. Sometimes these take the form of cryptograms. Here are two, the first related to the masks and the second to the beard that adorns it.

(Mask): *Tulimu ntumbukutu taw susanya ndoku*, that is: 'In the forest there are two beasts, one is a *ndoko*, the other a *ntumbukutu*. Their faces resemble each other but they are not identical.'

(Beard, called Mandefu): *Kwali tatale wantuga nwelu zabukulu bunena*, which means: 'A young man in conversation with one of the elders said: "you show me your beard, but my father has one also".'

The sense of the two proverbs is complementary: 'You say you are experienced because you have a beard, but my father, he also has one. You both seem the same, and yet you are different. The fact that you have a beard does not make you more intelligent than me.'

The ivory masks are small, in general about 5 ins.

64. Bena Lulua statuette of painted wood. Height
8 ins. ex-Belgian Congo.

65. Terracotta vase of the Mangbetu
(in the ex-Anglo-Egyptian Sudan). Height 11 ins.

66. Wooden seat from the Manyema region (between Lualaba and Tanganyika). Height 1 ft. 8 ins.

67. Detail of Plate 66.

68. Wooden mask called Kalagama. Height about 7 ins. (The holes pierced beneath the chin are for the beard.) Warega.

69. Loom with box in inlaid wood. Length 11 ins.
Batshioko, Angola.

70. Statuette of a woman in wood with traces of colour.
Before the first half of the 17th century. Height 1 ft.
North-West Angola.

71. Mambanda anthropocephalic wooden comb. 8 ins. Rhodesia.

high, and are decoratively incised. In particular, we find a series of rings with a central point, a *motif* that is also found in the ivory statuettes. In the wider field, this *motif* belongs to the symbology of archaic civilisations and is invariably found on ivory objects whose magic power it served to augment.

The statuettes of the Warega vary from 3 ins. to 4 ins. They depict the human figure in a standing position, either with the full complement of limbs, etc.; or in a stylised form, in which the neck and trunk merge in a single unit, on which are grafted the lower limbs without, however, any sign of arms. A severer stylisation is displayed in examples in which the body is reduced to a single pillar surmounted by a head; this type has a wide range of morphological variants and sub-variants.

Southern Congolese art, and that of northern Angola, show points of contact. Nevertheless, the productions of the Batshioko, whose name presents twenty-five variants and is the cause of great confusion among scholars, have a highly personal character.*

Fearless and cruel warrior races migrated to the Congo during the sixteenth century from the south-east, such as the Baluba, who were under pressure from the Dschagga. Their art displays common ethnic characteristics, and their sculptures reveal an aggressive force. The facial expressions on the human figure are fierce. The lineaments are strongly delineated, and the chisel-work is firm. Plastic relief is created by the powerful play of light and shade.

In contradistinction to the common convention which emphasises the head before the other parts of the body, the head in these statues is reduced to normal proportions and placed on an elongated trunk. The beard is forked, or slightly rounded, with no moustaches, the general effect being slightly Asiatic. The limbs, though crudely treated, express great strength. The knuckles of the hands are

* A piece described as 'Bashioko' in one museum can be called 'Watschiwokwe' in another, 'Kioko' in a third, and so on, albeit meaning the same tribe.

singly sculpted, as is also the case among the Bakuba. The head-dresses are elaborate, with heavy superstructures. The position of the body is always forceful, even when the person is shown seated. No benevolent or kindly feelings are projected from these images that seem like a taut spring about to be released.

The masks are much the same, the use of human hair contributing to a sense of *gravitas*. The chairs are supported by human or animal figures. There is an interesting wooden musical instrument with an elaborate geometrical design in which appears a female head with ox ears, which bears a striking resemblance to the Egyptian Hathor (Plate 69).

From the north-western regions of Angola come two female statuettes which are among the most ancient examples of African wooden sculpture that have come down to us. They date from before the first half of the seventeenth century. Towards the end of that century they were brought into Italy from Portugal by Cardinal Giorgio Cornaro of Padua. They later became the property of the Vallisnieri, and are to-day in the Ethnographic Museum in Rome. Their height is respectively 12 ins. and 11½ ins.; as they are similar, only one, the larger and better preserved, is reproduced here (Plate 70).

The convention of reproducing the breasts emerging from the sides of the arms is exemplified in this piece, a device we have noted among the Bayaka. The symbolic gesture of supporting the breasts with the hands, typical of the Mother Goddess, was achieved while at the same time leaving the breasts visible. The face, which is spherical, has a certain sweetness very different from the sculpture of the Batshioko: the hair is parted in the centre of the forehead and emerges from under a weighty head-dress; the neck is a trifle short, but nevertheless clearly indicated. The lower limbs are lacking, and the piece is mounted on a pedestal which bears rough ink marks inscribed in the eighteenth century. The modernity of these pieces is a valid testimony to the vitality of ancient African wooden sculpture. In the example here reproduced the hands are indicated, albeit schematically, while in the other statue the arms are truncated, like stumps.

As regards the area of West Africa's artistic influence, Carl Einstein holds that it extended as far as the Zambesi. And in fact the Masubia masks from the upper Zambesi share the characteristics already noted in corresponding Baluba productions. The geometrical contrast of the mouth in relation to the linear curves of the face is less accentuated than in the Baluba masks, but nevertheless still evident.

As for northern Rhodesia, we shall limit ourselves to mentioning a hair comb of the Mambunda, surmounted by a female face which, although stylised, recalls the Hathorian *motif* of the Batshioko musical instrument (Plate 71).

7

MINOR BRONZE AND GOLD WORK

West Africa's gold deposits have been justly termed legendary. They gave their name to the whole area known as 'The Gold Coast' whence a thriving gold trade was developed with European merchants. The outcrops came from alluvial soil which was for the most part composed of rocky remnants of the original strata. A series of washings —the method common to gold diggers everywhere—was used to collect the gold which came away in minute particles and was traded in this form under the somewhat inexact description of 'gold dust'. The mines, whose whereabouts were a state secret, produced nuggets of various sizes. These were considered inferior to the 'dust' because of their numerous impurities.

The kingdoms that flourished along the Gold Coast found in gold the best means of embellishing their courts. Travellers returned with details of the golden jewellery worn by the sovereigns and their courtiers. They spoke of an endless profusion of crowns, ear-rings, necklaces, pendants and bracelets. Weapons were inlaid with gold, and nearly everything from simple wooden objects to the insignia of rank was covered with gold leaf. The Chief Executioner wore a solid gold axe suspended from a chain round his neck, and other officials and important people were similarly accoutred.

The gold used for jewellery was of low carat, and the merchants who bartered guns, spirits, etc., for it called it 'fetish gold'. This may have been because the objects made from it were mostly fetish images; or it may simply have been a term of disparagement. Ornaments, amulets, pendants, are all enriched with decorative *motifs* reflecting ideas of symbolic magic. But in spite of this, the work has an explicitly aesthetic quality far exceeding that of other African productions, and is directly connected with the pleasure of self-adornment.

The method of applying gold leaf to wooden objects is not one that strictly comes under the head of the goldsmith's craft. Genuine jewellery is made either by *cire perdue* or by hammering. Among objects produced by these two methods there is a mask of the human face (Plate 72), which is unique in size and character. It is 7 ins. high and weighs 3½ lb. It comes from the treasure of the Ashanti king, Koffee-Kalkalli, and is without doubt a real portrait. It was taken to England in 1873, and described as 'a funeral mask in pure gold; used at the death of a tribal chieftain, the effigy being buried with the body'.

In his work on 'fetish gold' Charles Ratton suggests that the mask may be one of those mentioned by Rattray in the story of the Gyaman king, Adinkira, who had a gold throne made for himself in imitation of the king of the Ashanti. The latter was angry at having his throne copied, declared war on Adinkira, defeated him and cut his head off. The offending throne was then melted down and the gold used to make a pair of masks of the dead Adinkira. They were hung, one on either side of the Ashanti throne. A ring has been discovered behind the beard, which shows that it must have been hung upside down. This could well refer to the treatment reserved for a defeated enemy, and would support the theory that it is in fact one of Adinkira's masks. It was produced by *cire perdue*, and is a masterpiece of realism comparable to the best Mycenaean work.

The pendants and other jewels are of delicate filigree work. A tracery of curves and criss-cross lines in the finest gold thread forms 'arabesque' patterns, although the resemblance to Arab technique is purely superficial. The gold thread is all of a piece with the object: it is neither applied after the piece has been cast, nor in any way worked separately. The goldsmiths were able to produce a thread of well-proportioned and extremely fine wax, and with this they created the spirals and ornamental curves which characterise this jewellery. When we described the technique of *cire perdue* we saw how the model was covered with clay, into which the metal was poured to assume the impress which the wax had left on the clay. The central jewel in Plate G is a perfect example of this technique. It looks exactly as though the gold thread had been worked separately and then soldered: one would never guess it had been cast as a melted piece.

The Ashanti artists developed a variety of designs ranging from the simple to the baroque, elaborated on the basic form of the disk. The centre was sometimes filled with floral *motifs* surrounded by geometrical patterns. Sometimes the background was occupied by crocodiles depicted from above, while the empty spaces were covered with dotted lines—perhaps in obedience to that *horror vacui* which often impels the primitive artist to fill in every empty space. These dotted lines take the form of crosses, triangles and zig-zags. They are undoubtedly symbolic, although it is difficult to say of what.

The Baule called a pendant shaped like a plaque, *fawa*, or 'dish'—from the resemblance that it bears to the dish of a pair of balances. There are other jewels in the form of stars with eight or twelve points, or else in rectangles or squares. Those with points sticking out all round, known as 'sea urchins' or 'chestnut husks' are particularly interesting. There is a coloured reproduction of one of them in Plate G.

The Baule and Agni, as well as other small tribes descended from the Ashanti, make pendants out of small human masks. The use among such tribes of ritual wooden masks in their dances is undoubtedly due to the plastic influence of the Senufo and the Guro. These larger masks, which are of course of greater importance, inspired the diminutive mask-pendants. They too have a ritual value, besides their use as amulets. There is an aura of sophistication about them. The features, although a little stylised, are reproduced with extreme care, especially the hairs of the beard and the eyebrows. The chin is generally receding; the nose is rather prominent, and the eyes are indicated by small convex slits not unlike coffee beans. The hair and the beard are represented by means of little sticks of gold that circle the head and in some cases look not unlike the rays of the sun. These pendants vary in length from 1½ ins. to 4 ins. (Plate 73). They usually consist simply of an isolated human face, although there are examples in which the face is supported by a solar disk or a half-moon. The last is of particular interest when compared with the head-pieces of the funerary statues of the Bakota.

A rare example of this type of pendant shows stylised rams' horns which Ratton relates to lunar cults (Plate 74). Here also the body of the object appears to be composed entirely of gold thread, which harmonises with the subtle abstraction of the forms and produces a sense of lightness— almost of being diaphanous.

Jewels were inspired by other animals: the tortoise, the scorpion, the serpent, the leopard, various birds, etc. There is, for instance, the finely worked pendant reproducing three elephant masks, which is almost baroque in its elaboration of detail. If held horizontally the elephants resemble three snails. They are enriched with 'arabesque' designs and small birds (Plate G).

The Ashanti had a periodical feast called the Feast of Gold, connected with sexual rites at which such pendants were worn, a man's worldly wealth being indicated by the number of pendants hung about him. The bracelets and rings are rather heavy and show Arab influence. The bezel of the ring is sometimes decorated with a lion or a design shaped like a cupola. It is notable that, from the point of view of quality, Ashanti work results in a clearer tone of gold than does that of the Baule.

Embossed work mainly took the form of large disks or cylindrical boxes for amulets (Plate G). These boxes were worn round the neck or attached to a person's clothing. Leather objects were frequently covered with thin sheets of very finely chased gold.

As we have noted, the Ahanti kings had the monopoly of gold, and the goldsmiths—whose skills were handed down from father to son—formed a part of the hereditary nobility. Apart from their eminently decorative function and service as amulets, gold jewels were also used as a means of exchange, although natural gold in the form of 'gold dust' was more generally preferred. The precious particles were kept in special bronze vessels called *kuduo* (Plate 75). These were ancient ritual vases like the 'Cup of the Spirits' already described, used by the king in propitiation ceremonies.

These vessels bring us to what we have called the 'minor bronze work', in order to distinguish it from the well-known classical work of Benin and of the Yoruba cycle. It is a somewhat unsatisfactory term since the *kuduo* themselves are works of major importance. Ritually they are related to a species of ancient Italian vase, known as the *cista*, and to the Egyptian and Mesopotamian *situla*. In the latter, winged spirits are often depicted sprinkling the holy water with an *aspersorium* in the form of a pine cone. Each drop symbolised regeneration and corresponded to the seed of a pine tree.

In the ceremony described above, the *kuduo* was used to hold the water which the king, in a symbolic action, spat out around him. Egyptian *situlae* held the lustral water used in purificatory ceremonies, and were moreover enriched with a set of values acquired from their connection with the food offerings made for the dead. Under this aspect they became one of the instruments used in funerary ceremonial. The *kuduo* were originally cult vessels used for purificatory purposes, or to hold the offerings destined for *ntoro*, the male principle present in every human being.

In externals, the similarity between the *kuduo* and the ancient Italian *cista* is quite striking. There are corresponding ornamental figures on the lid, and similar *motifs* engraved round the sides. The figures are either symbolically connected with special Ashanti rites or events in

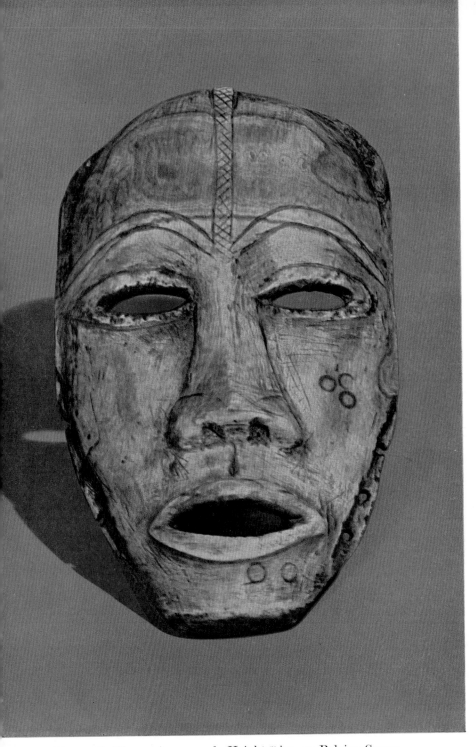

PLATE F. Warega ivory mask. Height 7 ins. ex-Belgian Congo.

Ashanti history, or they are plastic illustrations of well-known proverbs. Paulme, the author of an interesting study of such illustrations, explains the *motif* of a chief surrounded by musicians as an expression of the saying, 'a chief is never alone'.

Sometimes the *motifs* are distinctly macabre and refer to human sacrifice. An example of this is the reproduction of the lower jaw of an individual who has been tortured. It was the custom to detach the jaws from the cranium of a sacrificial victim, and to leave them for several days on the altar, in order to prevent the spirit of the dead person from returning and seeking whom it might devour in revenge.

The shape of a *kuduo* varies. There is a box type; and there is one shaped like a vase which swells out at the base, narrows at the middle and widens again towards the mouth. And all the types are supported by small feet. They were produced by means of *cire perdue*, as were the other minor bronze works of the Ashanti and the Baule, notably the well-known weights called *mrammuo* which were used to weigh the 'gold dust'.

Many of these weights are enlivened by a sense of fantasy and a subtle vein of humour. Like the Egyptian hieroglyphs, they provide a fund of information about various human activities, technical instruments and the morphology of animals and plants. They are both anthropomorphic and theriomorphic. They run into complicated fractions, the smallest being far less than an ounce, and the largest about 2½ lb. The subjects treated can be divided as follows:

A. *Human figures, single or in groups.* In many pieces after the colonial period we find a chief depicted on his throne. The body is no longer rigidly schematised, but assumes a variety of relaxed poses. The basic formula, however, is still schematic. Single figures also represent different trades and professions, from the Chief Executioner with his large scimitar, to the warrior armed with musket and flint. Sometimes humans are associated with horses or other domestic animals found round a farm. Grouped figures include representations of the two legendary friends Amoako and Adu, who are shown warmly embracing as they find each other after a long separation. This *motif* is also found on *kuduo* lids. Sometimes we find a mother and child, or working people busy with pestle and mortar, or execution scenes. Anthropomorphic demons like Sasabonsam, who jumps down from a tree and attacks passers-by, are rarer. Another subject is provided by musicians, particularly figures beating gongs.

B. *Parts of the human body.* These were used to form submultiples in the scale of weights. The head is the commonest feature and recalls the diminutive gold masks, even if the bronze, which is less ductile than gold, does not lend itself to such fine workmanship.

c. *Zoomorphic figures.* These are divided into the various sorts of animal life found in the district. There are mammals, birds, fish, reptiles and insects. In the case of insects, as in small-scale vegetation *motifs*, the actual object itself is often used as a model. It is covered with clay, and precisely the same technique is employed as with *cire perdue.* The result is even more truly a cast taken 'from life'. Of the mammals, the elephant and the long-horned antelope appear most frequently, the antelope with its horns curved backwards until they touch its rump. There are also examples of the leopard, although very different from those found among the classical images of Benin. Here the beast is portrayed with its prey between its teeth (Plate 76), and its spotted hide is represented by small concentric rings; these were executed on the clay model with a wax filament. Another piece consists of three doves on a triangular perch, apparently drinking from a small basin. Sometimes the triangular object is supported by a short pillar. There is an elegant and stylised figure of a fish seen from above (Plate 77); it has a large head and a curved tail. Other fish, however, tend to be round and flat. The crocodile, which is called *mtanu*, is distinguished by its large coarse scales, and it too is sometimes shown with its prey between its jaws. A *motif* common to both weights and gold necklaces is that of the serpent in the form of a rolled spiral with the head protruding from one end. The scorpions (perhaps because they were modelled from life) are particularly realistic, shown with their fatal death sting unsheathed.

D. *Parts of animal.* These, like the parts of the human body, are used as submultiples. The head is the most frequent subject, such as that of the cock, goat and antelope; but we also find the tail of a fish. Stylistically, the heads show the influence of the sculpture of the wooden ritual masks, as is also evident in the corresponding pieces of goldsmith work.

E. *Vegetation motifs.* Here we find various kinds of trees, notably the palm; also the ground-nut plant and edible vegetation. There are ears of corn and there are seeds, which were the smallest unit of weight. The models in these instances were taken from life, as with the insects.

F. *Instruments.* The range is very wide, comprising craftsmen's tools, domestic articles and weapons. There is a hoe with a sort of moveable tongue, indicative of a developed farming technique (Plate 78). Besides other agricultural tools there are also the insignia of various trades, such as axes, knives, pincers, bellows, etc. Domestic items include chairs and a special sort of bench called *akonnua*; there are also scales, various containers or vessels, and lamps, etc. There are also musical instruments such as horns, gongs and drums. Weapons include the characteristic scimitar—a traditional weapon—as well as firearms, which are of course of European origin. Models of old cannons, muskets with flint-stones and powder kegs, are eloquent evidence of the sort of goods which the Gold Coast merchants offered in exchange for the precious gold objects and so-called 'gold dust'.

Most of the weights are in bronze, but there are rare examples to be found in silver and, in the royal treasury, in gold. They were often used as amulets or for decorative purposes, rather than as simple weights.

Some pieces appear to be imperfect: a human figure lacks an arm, or a fish a bit of its head; in others there are additions, such as bronze threads incorporated after the piece was cast. But this is not surprising since they are, after all, weights; and over and above 'artistic' requirements there was always the need to obtain an exact measurement. This measurement, however, was often relative since, as Kjersmeier observes, chiefs and powerful people—not to mention the king—used outsize weights in order that they should obtain larger measures. This is the origin of the Ashanti proverb which says: 'The weights of a chief are not the same as those of poor folk.' On the oldest weights there are symbols in the form of spirals, pyramids, swastikas, etc., and some of these are also to be found on the gold pieces.

Our brief survey of the so-called 'minor' bronzes finds a fitting conclusion in the animal reproduced in Plate 79. It comes from the Grassland in the Cameroons, and was produced by means of *cire perdue*. It has not been precisely identified but is full of a singularly expressive power. It exudes a repulsive aggressiveness, as though it were indeed alive and caught in the very moment of gathering itself for the kill. The lean body accentuates the large head with its enormous eyes and half-opened lids. The sense of its being about to pounce is admirably captured in the position of the limbs, and in the tail which is flexed sideways. To me it has always seemed one of the strangest and most powerful of the minor African bronzes. This examination should have shown that in the minor golden and bronze works an ancient tradition was able to maintain both technical skill and artistic sensibility at an almost constant level.

8

THE INFLUENCE OF NEGRO ART

It is well known that in the twentieth century Western art has been directly influenced by the so-called 'primitive' arts of Africa and the Pacific islands. The origins of this influence and the precise course it took are, however, rather more obscure.

France assumes a role of capital importance. She provided a haven for the art rebels of every nation. She was like a cauldron in which the elements of vital reaction met and coalesced. Already in Gauguin we can see the first symptoms of the modern artist's impelling need to flee from his own civilisation in order to revitalise his art in contact with one closer to nature. He wanted to wash his clothes, not in the little stream running at the foot of the garden, but in the wide sea, among people for whom myth was still a living reality, and for whom the old pagan gods still survived. By this means he sought to achieve a catharsis of his whole being. He wanted to escape from the ossified forms in which he had been born, and to absorb the fluid forces of life still valid for those willing to submit to them. This trend towards the exotic—not confined solely to Africa and the Pacific—is the substrate experience from which modern Western art in its various manifestations has sprung.

The beginnings of this movement can be placed even earlier. As Alberto Savino perceptively observes:

It is not difficult to trace the origins of Negro influence in French art to the death of Louis XIV. This marked the beginning of the decadence of the state as a moral entity. *L'état c'est moi* stands as the definition of a 'closed' society. There was clearly no place for black idols of the Congo among the bewigged scholars of the sultanate of Versailles, such as Racine and Boileau. France's cultural forces were still directed inwards. But the fact remains that whatever the decorative virtues may be of President Lebrun in full regalia of tail-coat and opera hat, he lacks the terrible qualities of the war god of Dahomey in the ethnographic museum of the Trocadéro, loaded with arms and looking rather like a bird whose feathers have been ruffled the wrong way. And many Frenchmen, among them those eminent in society and letters, have ended by preferring the latter to the former.

But leaving aside diverting paradoxes such as this, we must try to determine the causal value that a piece of African sculpture had for a European artist. The reactionary process at the beginning of the century consisted of disparate tendencies: there was a spirit of revolt, but no goal. At this point the discovery of African art acted as a kind of catalyst. Catalysis, as we know, is a process whereby an element in a given situation operates as an agent of change while itself remaining essentially unaffected by the process which it has set in motion. African art acted on European art in precisely this way. Although created for quite different purposes, it dynamised the process of artistic reaction and provided a *nodus* around which it could take place. It revitalised aesthetic values and indicated an immediate goal, together with the steps necessary to achieve it. But it remained outside the process. The vital ritual value of the masks and statues was ignored. What the European artist experienced was a purely emotional stimulus derived from the synthesis or abstraction of forms, the achitectonics of planes, or the predominance of the sphere over the cube. Unlike Guillaume Apollinaire, they did not realise that Negro sculpture consists of abstractions of a supernatural character that have been given to it by the artists who sculpted it, and by the believers who paid homage to it.

But the interaction between these art worlds was also effective at a deeper level than that of purely formal resemblance. As Raffaele Carrieri has justly noted, an African mask can achieve new factive vitality after it has been filtered through the individual sensibility, by generating for example, a landscape or a still life.

The question arises, whether it is possible to discover the actual moment of birth when Negro art began to influence modern art. Rather surprisingly, it is. And given the historic importance of the occasion we will let Maurice Vlaminck speak for himself, for to him more than to anyone else we owe our knowledge of the initial stages of this influence.

One afternoon in the year 1905 I found myself in Argenteuil. I was painting the Seine, with its boats and small hills beyond. The sun was blazing. I gathered my paints and brushes together, picked up my canvas, and went into a nearby inn. Sailors and coal-heavers were standing at the bar. While I was refreshing myself with white wine and Sedlitz water, I noticed on a little table, among bottles of Pernod, absinthe and curaçao, three pieces of Negro sculpture: two Dahomey statuettes daubed with red, yellow and white ochre, and another from the Ivory Coast, which was black.

Was it perhaps because I had been working for two or three hours in the full sunlight? Or was it the particular state of mind I happened to be in that day? Or perhaps it was due to my preoccupation with certain problems of my own? Whatever it was, these three statuettes had the most profound effect on me. In a moment of intuition I became aware of their latent power; and all Negro art was in that moment revealed to me.

And yet Derain and I were already well acquainted with the Trocadéro: we had explored it from end to end on several occasions. We knew it thoroughly. We had conscientiously studied everything it contained. But neither of us had ever seen in the objects there exhibited anything beyond what convention regards as barbaric fetishes. The meaning of an instinctive art such as this had always eluded us.

But the three Negro statuettes in that inn at Argenteuil meant more to me even than this. They affected me at the deepest possible level.

I asked the landlord to sell them to me. He began by refusing. I persisted, and, after many hesitations, refusals and excuses, he gave them to me, on condition that I bought a considerable quantity of his red wine. When I had done this I was able, at last, to carry the statues away with me.

Shortly afterwards, one of my father's friends to whom I had shown the statues, offered to give me some pieces of his own, which his wife had threatened to throw on the rubbish heap. I called on him and came away with a large white mask and two superb statues from the Ivory Coast. I hung the white mask above my bed. I was elated, but at the same time somehow disturbed: I felt I was in the presence of all the primitivism and all the grandeur latent in Negro art. When Derain arrived, and saw the white mask, he was speechless. He seemed to be stunned, and immediately offered me twenty francs for it, which I refused. Eight days later he offered me fifty; and happening to have no money that day, I accepted. He took the object away with him and hung it on the wall in his studio in the Rue Tourlaque. When Picasso and Matisse saw it, they in their turn were bowled over by it in just the same way. From that day the hunt for Negro art was on!

We could hardly ask for better evidence than this, or for a more fitting 'birth place'; for we are in France at the beginning of this century, and the witness is one of the leaders of the imminent artistic revolution. But although Vlaminck played an important part in introducing his contemporaries to Negro art he was not directly influenced by it himself, as were Derain, Matisse and Picasso, to mention three of the earliest.

72. Ashanti gold mask. Height 7 ins.

73. Ashanti gold pendants.
Heights: $2\frac{1}{2}$ ins.; $1\frac{1}{2}$ ins.; 3 ins.; 2 ins.; $2\frac{1}{4}$ ins.

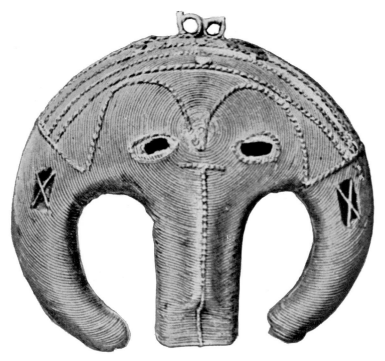

74. Baule gold pendant in the form of a stylised ram's head.
Width 3½ ins. Ivory Coast.

75. Bronze vessel (*Kuduo*) to hold gold-dust. Height 1 ft. 2 ins. Ashanti, Ghana. (From the house of the Queen regnant, aunt of Prempeh I ad Ajesu.)

76. Gold weight in bronze. Width 3 ins. Baule. Ivory Coast.

77. Gold weight in bronze. Length 3 ins. Baule,
Ivory Coast.

78. Gold weight in bronze. Length $2\frac{1}{2}$ ins. Baule,
Ivory Coast.

79. Animal in bronze. Length 7 ins. Height 3½ ins. Cameroons.

The Influence of Negro Art

Bernard Berenson drew attention to Matisse's interest in archaic and 'primitive' art as long ago as 1904 in the pages of *The Nation*. He had intervened on the artist's behalf, protesting against the abuse to which his work was being subjected. In 1906 we see Matisse acquiring Negro objects, and he has left us his own account of the following incident.

> At that time I used to pass Father Sauvage's shop in the Rue de Rennes, where some Negro statuettes were on show in the window. I was moved by their purity of line, and by their strangeness. There was a beauty about them, not unlike that of Egyptian art. I bought one of them and showed it to Gertrude Stein, whom I happened to be going to see that day. While we were looking at it, Picasso came in. He at once became enthusiastic, and from then on everyone began to look for Negro statues, which in those days were not difficult to find.

According to Diehl, the piece Matisse acquired that day was a Negro mask that reminded him of an Egyptian head in red porphyry that he had seen in the Louvre. That mask marked the beginning of his African collection and of his *fauve* period which, as Paul Fierens remarks, shows an influence midway between that of the Egyptian-Roman portraits of Fayum, and Negro masks. K. Asplund, moreover, points out that the profound influence exerted by Matisse at this time was of a piece with the revelatory discovery of Negro art.

As a matter of aesthetic principle, Matisse was always in search of foreign stimulus. As he once said to Apollinaire: 'I have never avoided the influence of others. I should have considered it a form of cowardice and of disloyalty towards myself. I believe that the artist's personality develops and asserts itself in conflict with other personalities. If the conflict proves fatal, and it goes under, that simply means that it was fit for nothing better.' On which Apollinaire comments: 'As a result, all plastic expression—the hieratic Egyptians, the refined Greeks, the voluptuous Cambodians, ancient Peruvian productions, and African Negro statuettes can interest an artist and help him to develop his own personality, in proportion to the passion that they have inspired in him.'

In 1906 Picasso's excitement was aroused by Matisse's Negro mask, and in 1907 he painted his celebrated picture, *Les Demoiselles d'Avignon.* The relation between the two events is essential to an understanding of this picture, in which the Negro—or alternatively, the Spanish—influence is still very much a subject of discussion. Picasso himself, however, has told Zervos that in 1907 he was still ignorant of African art; and Zervos says: 'It was some time later that he experienced his revelation of Negro art. One day, coming out of the Museum of Comparative Sculpture, which in those days occupied the left wing of the Trocadéro Palace, he was inquisitive enough to push open the door into the rooms of the old Ethnographic Museum. Even to-day, more than twenty years later (1942) and in spite of those contemporary events which have disturbed him so profoundly, Picasso still speaks with deep emotion of the shock he received that day from the sight of those African sculptures.' From this account it would appear that Picasso had forgotten the mask he saw at Derain's. Although of lesser importance than the declared Spanish influence on *Les Demoiselles,* the influence of the African piece is nevertheless still perceptible.

Apollinaire was introduced to African art by Vlaminck, Derain and Matisse. He owned the famous 'Bird of Benin'— a term he was to use as a nickname for Picasso in *Poète Assassiné.* The audacity of Picasso's *Les Demoiselles,* which was dubbed a 'philosophic bawdy house', and in which nothing survived of the preceding blue and rose period, was not accepted by Apollinaire. He used Marcel Adema's words when he said that the women's faces appeared one morning 'like grinning Congo idols'; but Apollinaire's own view of Negro art was clear: he affirmed that it required aesthetic courage to consider these idols as true works of art.

Picasso's picture was the result of long months of experiment. It shattered traditional schemes of design and composition, and marks a decisive development in modern painting. The frontal projection of the eye in the left-hand figure is reminiscent of Egyptian methods, while the figures on the right have obviously been influenced by Congo masks.

According to Mme Buffet-Picabia, Picasso 'found his way by means of Negro sculpture. The works of 1907-08 are unequivocal evidence of this, and have therefore been called his 'Negro' period. The 'Ballerina' of 1907 (Plate 80), has clearly been inspired by the funerary images of the Bakota (Plate 50). The 'Head' painted in the same period was influenced by the Ivory Coast masks and by the Congo, as are also a whole series of drawings and sketches published by Zervos. Negro art also made itself felt in this period, which could properly be called 'pre-cubist', in Picasso's wooden sculptures such as the 'Bambola' (Plate 81) and the 'Man Standing'. The resolution and reorganisation of planes, the synthesis of forms reduced to their essentials, the limbs either merged in the statue or only summarily sculpted, are all elements of the purest African tradition.

In painting, apart from formal values, there are of course chromatic ones. African influence is again evident in Picasso's use of polychrome streaks. Valminck says that his method of painting his assemblages of forms in black and yellow ochre was that of the Negroes when making their *tapas* and their fetishes.

The next period brings us to 'protocubism' where Picasso's Protean abilities found new fields for their exercise; but the African experience remained among the most significant and the most fruitful. Many artists find the strength to express their own interior states, previously vague and ill-defined, by comparing their artistic assumptions with those of a master, and thereby achieving a constant renewal of their personal experience. This 'renewal day by day' admirably epitomises the course which

Picasso's dynamic and revolutionary work has taken. As he himself has said: 'To copy others is inevitable, but to copy yourself—what humiliation!'

Another of the great moderns to be partially influenced by African art was Constantin Brancusi, who arrived in Paris in 1904 from his native Rumania. Intolerant and proud, he disdained any form of publicity; but the extra-ordinary inner strength of this humble peasant's son left its mark on all who met him. His aloofness kept him apart from 'schools' or 'movements': the stages of his artistic development were the product of long meditation endured in the solitude of his *atelier*. His peculiar contribution was, as Cardnuff Ritchie has observed, 'that of fusing—by means of Rumanian popular tradition—the barbaric intensity of African and prehistoric sculpture with the occult sophistica-tion of Indian and Chinese work'.

Rejecting what he called 'beefsteak sculpture' which, according to him, had dominated the period from Michel-angelo to Rodin, Brancusi worked with the force latent in the material itself. 'The Kiss' (1908) consists of two people merged together in a block of hard stone. The influence of 'primitive art' is already discernible. However, the first distinctively African work is 'The Prodigal Son', executed in 1914. Here the confident resolution and reorganisation of planes, the abstract forms and the overall asymmetry which gives the effect of a constant striving for a point of equilibrium (quite apart from the actual material used, which is wood), all indicate a vital knowledge of Negro art. Later in his life Brancusi renewed this knowledge, or experience, in the form of the purest synthesis between it and Oriental art—a synthesis in which the Oriental influence is predominant.

In 1909, Brancusi met Modigliani whom he taught to sculpt. The desire to sculpt remained with Modigliani for most of his working life. The picture called 'Egyptian Bust' belongs to this year, in which the face bears all the marks of classical Modiglianesque sculpture. It is stylised and elongated and reminds one of the wooden sculpture of the

Western Sudan (Plate 83). As Carrieri points out. Modigliani had been introduced to African art in the preceding year, 1908, in the salon of the Independents. 'The Idol', which he exhibited there, is ample evidence of this. Modigliani was avid of the most disparate experiences which he then proceeded to make his own. Lionello Venturi, the celebrated art critic, describes how in Paris 'the experiences multiplied themselves: there was Negro sculpture, French Gothic sculpture, the Italian primitives, Japanese art and El Greco. These and other discordant voices from the past met in him [Modigliani], some speaking to his idealism and others to his sense of violence. Maud Dale has described how, when Negro art first began to influence the Montmartre group, Modigliani was already a sculptor. She says that the stone heads and various drawings of caryatids that he has left us show that, at that time, he was fully aware of the formal power of African sculpture.

Interest and curiosity in Negro art were stimulated by a scandal that exploded on Paris in 1911 in which, in spite of himself, Apollinaire became involved through his well-known collection of Negro sculpture and exotics. A sensation had been created by the theft of the 'Mona Lisa'. This was subsequently returned to its place; but the directors of the Louvre had at the same time discovered the loss of various other pieces. These consisted of statuettes, some of them quite precious examples of the Phoenician period. The author of these thefts turned out to be none other than Apollinaire's secretary-cum-amanuensis whom the poet knew simply as Pieret. He had been bringing the pieces to the house, where they had excited the admiration of Apollinaire and his friends, who had been given some of them as presents. These Phoenician statues, together with his African sculpture, constituted the most interesting part of the poet's collection. But when the directors of the Louvre announced the thefts Apollinaire began to grow suspicious. His suspicions were at once confirmed by Pieret himself, who modestly admitted his

guilt, but insisted that he deserved no particular credit for
what he had done, since it was so easy to steal objects from
the Louvre. Apollinaire hastily dismissed Pieret and
decided to return the missing pieces anonymously through
the *Paris-Journal*. Among the friends who had benefited
from these gifts was Picasso, and it was he who collected
all the pieces together and carried them in a suitcase to the
paper's editorial offices. In spite of these precautions,
however, the police succeeded in singling out Apollinaire
as having taken a leading part in the affair. The fact that
he was actually guilty of shielding the real criminal did
not make his position any easier, and he was put in prison.
It was only during the subsequent judicial enquiry that his
complete innocence of the thefts themselves was finally
established.

Another highly significant voice, destined to be tragically
silenced by the First World War, was that of Gaudier-
Brzeska. His works mark the effective close of the era of
academicism. They are characterised by an almost in-
credible maturity of expression: he was killed at twenty-
four. It is to terms such as 'cyclopean' or 'titanic' that one
turns when contemplating the extraordinary force and
energy inhabiting his work. Resolutely eschewing the
facile hedonism of the immediate past, he is intent solely
on impregnating the stone with the maximum possible
power. He was open to the influences of all the great ages of
sculpture. He studied Egyptian, African and Chinese work,
proving, as Pound puts it, that 'Hellenism, neo-Hellenism,
neo-Renaissancism and Albert Memorialism do not contain and circumscribe all that it is possible to know on
the subject'.

If the effigy which he made of his friend Ezra Pound, the
celebrated 'Hieratic Head', presents analogies with the
statues of Easter Island, and the 'Boy with Coney' mirrors
the products of the Chow dynasty, the 'Imp' (Plate 84)
shows an unmistakable African influence. It was one of
Gaudier's last works, made in 1914, a year before his
death at Neuville St Vaast. The elongated trunk is sup-

ported by lower limbs flexed in the manner of Baule works. The head is shown as stiffly turned on the neck; the features stand out slightly from the oval of the face as in Negro statuary. The hands and feet match the schematised lower limbs.

Gaudier was a member of the Vorticist movement, and in the first number of Wyndham Lewis's *Blast* (20th June, 1914) he published the Vorticist manifesto. After reviewing the artistic contributions of various civilisations, he ends thus:

Besides these highly developed peoples there lived in the world other races inhabiting Africa and the Ocean Islands.

When we first knew them they were very near the palaeolithic stage. Though they were not so much dependent upon animals their expenditure of energy was wide, for they began to till the land and practise crafts rationally; and they fell into contemplation before their sex: the site of their great energy: their convex maturity.

They pulled the sphere lengthways and made the cylinder, that is the vortex of fecundity, and it has left us the masterpieces that are known as love charms.

The soil was hard, material difficult to win from nature; storms frequent, as also fevers and other epidemics. They got frightened: this is the vortex of fear, its mass is the pointed cone, its masterpieces the fetishes.

And we the moderns: Epstein, Brancusi, Archipenko, Dunikowski, Modigliani, and myself, through the incessant struggle in the complex city, have likewise to spend much energy.

The knowledge of our civilisation embraces the world, we have mastered the elements.

We have been influenced by what we liked most, each according to his own individuality, we have crystallised the sphere into the cube, we have made a combination of all the possible shaped masses—concentrating them to express our abstract thoughts of conscious superiority.

Will and consciousness are our Vortex.

These diverse influences, the resolution and reorganisation of the form and its symbolic re-elaboration, are incorporated in an interesting piece made of green marble, an amulet that for some months Gaudier carried round his neck (Plate 85).

We have said that Negro art had the effect of a catalyst on the development of modern art, a comparison which presumes the existence of a *materia prima* in which the posited 'chemical' reaction could take place. This *materia prima* was simply the group of highly talented individuals who happened to find themselves at work at more or less the same time, on more or less the same problems. In this chapter we have named some of these artists and outlined some aspects of their work. But as the sound of an explosion reverberates long after the immediate impact has been made of hammer on gunpowder, so the effects of Negro art have continued to make themselves felt long after the initial impetus has been expended. Individuals and movements submitted to its influence for years after the events described in this chapter. Surrealism was affected by it. As Savinio observes: 'The surrealist seeks mystery, loves wonder, desires fear. A Negro idol induces an attitude of receptivity. Before it, we aspire to a condition of sacred terror such as a native of the Congo will experience. And who knows but that one day he may indeed receive such an experience? Who knows whether he has not already done so?'

In Germany, the works of both Pechstein and Schmidt-Rottluff shows to what extent it is possible to absorb the stylistic canons and techniques of Negro sculpture. Rottluff's 'Head', which is illustrated in Plate 86, derives from African art not only in the composition of the face but also in the matter of actual technique, the wood being worked

Plate G. Golden jewelry from Ghana. Pendant with three elephants' heads ($3\frac{1}{4}$ ins. long); cylindrical container for amulets; pendant ($3\frac{1}{2}$ ins. high); ear-ring.

by sculpting it into very small facets as if it were a Senufo mask.

We cannot end without at least mentioning 'Dada', the other reactionary movement. But the African influence in 'Dada' is too slight to be worth close attention. Like other minor manifestations, it adds nothing essential to the story.

9

PRESENT AND FUTURE
DEVELOPMENTS

We shall conclude this study of African art with an assessment of contemporary conditions and possible future lines
of development.

Contemporary African art is itself a misleading phrase.
There are artistic activities carried on by Africans; but
there is little essential connection (although there is some
superficial resemblance) between these and the ancient
African traditions. The process of psychological disintegration goes back a long way. It was the iconoclastic
influence of Islam that first impinged destructively on
African concepts. Areas of moral debilitation, natural in
so old a people, facilitated the process of disruption. Too
often, Africans no longer seemed capable of defending their
own 'creed' in the face of external pressure. Such spontaneous outbreaks of self-assertion as occurred were
sporadic, even if vehement and cruel.

For an African to defend his art is more than to defend
his cultural patrimony: it is to defend his very essence—
his soul. No 'Custodian of the Fine Arts' could have pro-
tected these values. They were jealously enshrined in the
individual soul as a legacy of the remotest ages, and were
guarded there. The value of such an 'artistic' attitude
should have been made plain in the preceding pages; but
it is still important to bear in mind the fundamental
difference between the spirits animating African art and
Western art, that is between the creation of ritual instruments and of *objets d'art.*

The object created by the African was a manifestation of
the world of magic. It was the spatial testimony of his

vision of the world, the tangible expression of his faith. The survival of his tradition, and therefore of his civilisation, hung on it. It was the *sine qua non* of his whole way of life. At a certain period in history, internal disintegration was accelerated by that most disruptive of all forces, colonialism. The reports of early navigators, and the results of intrepid individual explorers, confirmed the fact that the Black Continent contained fabulous riches. The various European nations contested the control of strategic maritime routes and displayed unedifying rivalry in their exploitation of the slave trade, each vying bitterly with the other in the struggle to obtain the most advantageous foothold. Although this is not the place for a disquisition on colonialism, attention must be firmly drawn to the discrepancy between the humanitarian façade, and the actuality of looting and exploitation which colonisation all too often entailed, and which sufficiently revealed its true aims.

Administrators were placed in positions of responsibility for which they were totally unprepared. Confronted with difficult situations they all used one language, that of the whip and the gun. But rudimentary methods such as these tended to produce precisely the opposite results to what was intended. The colonisers' dreams of domination were jarred by violent reactions and the consolidation of nationalistic feeling. The 'hard-system' was even then not discarded; but a psychological complement was found in the systematic *denaturalising* of the indigenous people and in depriving them of their traditional spiritual patrimony.

The 'authorities' outlawed the secret societies on the pretext that they were used for political purposes and contrary to the interests of the occupying power. They suspended tribal rituals on the grounds that they were of dubious morality. They cast continual ridicule on the notion of ancestor worship. The natural result was that the subject race was left with a pronounced inferiority complex.

Signs of this trauma soon became evident in the arts, which went into an abrupt decline. At this juncture, the influence of the missionaries, who invariably followed in the wake of the colonisers, was unrelievedly harmful. They neither gave (nor asked for) any quarter in the struggle against 'paganism'. Thousands of wooden sculptures were consigned to the flames as unclean fetishes, while a new ethical system gave rise to hitherto inconceivable ideas of guilt and sin occasioned by the simple fact of physical nudity.

Africans were faced with a direct choice: either they could remain faithful to their old ways, which would mean persecution; or they could embrace the coloniser and seek to derive from him what practical benefits they could. Many chose the path of personal advantage in the hope of finding favour with whoever happened to be ruling their country. In saying this, it is far from my intention to cast doubt on the good faith of individual conversions, or on the sincerity of the missionaries who were obviously convinced of the necessity and justice of their actions. The judgements passed in this book on the episode of colonialism are confined simply and solely to its effect on African art.

In most cases, conversion was a very superficial affair. New ideas of God, of the saints and martyrs, blended with elements from the tribal pantheon to produce an effect of personal syncretism. The rise of the so-called 'Black Churches' was the occasion for an iconoclastic fervour in which, in their onslaughts on their own heritage, the colonised peoples exceeded even the missionaries themselves. Among the Bakongo for instance, Simon Kibangu, whose personal influence was extraordinary, persuaded all the neighbouring tribes to follow his example and destroy their pagan sculpture.

Wherever the indigenous races fail to have recourse to fanatical outbursts of this sort, it is fair to assume that the new faith has not succeeded in replacing the old, or that it has not struck so deep. The malleable feminine element in the African character, apparently so easy to convert, has pursued its private syncretic adjustment of the old to the new faith.

Present and Future Developments

A corresponding process has occurred elsewhere. As Gauguin tells us in writing of Tahiti: 'The gods of former days find a haven in the memories of the women. It is a strangely moving sight to see, little by little, the national gods stirring in Tahura—thrusting aside the veils under which the missionaries have buried them. In brief, the catechists have had an extremely superficial effect. Their instruction has been like a thin coating of enamel which flakes and comes away before the least promptings of intelligence.'

As we have seen, art in Africa was a direct offshoot of religion. It is therefore not surprising that these proselytising activities, together with the continual attacks on the essential motives of the various African religions, should be reflected in African art.

Their faith destroyed, their courts abolished, African artists were deprived of their mainspring. In 1927, when Georges Hardy had become aware of the total decadence of Negro art, he wrote: 'To-day after a century of struggle between Africa and Europe, there is a void or near-void.' And the void to which he refers is, as we have seen, a moral vacuum which the Europeans have been incapable of filling. They have replaced the original vital faith with stucco saints and insipid oleographs, so that Rémy de Gourmont could say with truth: 'L'art religieux est mort.'

The local princely courts used in the old days to stimulate artistic activity. They were embellished by works of the best craftsmen. Now the market is the European tourist, and the general level of taste has sunk accordingly. William Fagg cites as an example of this the case of the Nigerian sculptor Bagomboye of Odo-Owa, who up till ten years ago was sculpting in the traditional manner and producing works of fine quality for use at tribal ceremonials. His technical and artistic abilities attracted the attention of the British authorities, who appointed him to teach sculpture in the government school of Omu-Aran. It was not long before his inspiration began to flag. Fortunately he retained his technical virtuosity, with which he could satisfy the demands of the European market for 'African-style' objects in the form of book-ends, paper-knives and caryatids. When he was asked why he had stopped sculpting in the traditional manner, he replied simply: 'The Europeans pay me because I make what they ask for. Why therefore should I make anything else?'

This is happening all over Africa. The patronage of the court of Dahomey maintained families of artists with specific skills that had been handed down from father to son. There were the Zado who were commissioned to make the royal thrones; and the Huntondji who were special goldsmiths employed by the nobility, and were themselves of exalted rank. Such artists depended for their livelihood on a certain social order. When this crumbled, they had either to adapt themselves and produce work suited to the tastes and proclivities of their new masters, or to change their profession.

Those artists who have chosen to emigrate to the countries of the various colonial powers are confronted with an even more complex situation. In Paris or London such *émigrés* visit various academies and exhibitions devoted to the fine arts. They learn a certain amount about different aspects of Western culture. Often they forget their own native speech, and adopt one or more of the European languages. It is only to be expected that the psychological effects of such cultural miscegenation should be apparent in the actual works of 'art' themselves.

Mr L. Wadiri provides a good example of what happens to an artist in this position. He belongs to the Ijaw tribe in which the mask illustrated in Plate D originated. He comes of a family of fishermen who boast a long tradition of canoe carving. After he had won a government award, he went to London, where he studies and sculpts, and where he has taken part in public exhibitions. His works show an assimilation of just those stylistic canons of modern art that have been derived from African art. In his work we can trace a reawakening of African art in many characteristic manifestations of the Western world, as in 'Jazz Scene' (Plate 87). There is an irony here. Young African negroes who come to the West to absorb our cultural experience are in fact searching for their own soul among those very people who have contributed to taking it away from them. This sojourning in foreign lands is perhaps comparable to what Maeterlinck described in 'The Blue Bird'. At my request, Mr Wadiri has made a summary, a sort of testament, of his artistic beliefs. This is what he says:

1. The aim of African Art is towards something other than the mere copying of nature. A relief or a wood-carving in the round may be drawn from the human figure, for it is only natural that the artist, in spite of himself, should transcribe something from actual nature. The 'what' is far more important than the 'how', as it has always been in the art of symbolic and significant representation—a representation of things that cannot be seen except by the imaginative.

2. Therefore, those who wish to study the 'development' of African art must entirely free themselves from the European tendency to use the observation of nature as a measuring rod to trace stylistic sequences. It can only be studied as showing at different times a greater or lesser degree of consciousness, energy, unity, grace, and the like, but never illusion.

3. However, today, after a century or so of stagnation through foreign influences, and in a generation where no human being is any longer himself, we are still striving to put to use the remains of our ancient faculty into our everyday activity.

The question is, could these ideas form a basis for the future development of African art? There seems little doubt that they will form an aspect of it, but a certain amount of dross would have to be eliminated before they could be considered as a 'platform'.

In Africa to-day, decolonisation is in process. The cry for 'a return to our origins' is merely one method of carrying the standard against the colonists. Reference to 'ancient traditions' and so on are intended to revive the hitherto quiescent 'African' consciousness. But it is not enough to recall the externals of these traditions without the original afflatus that animated them. In short, there can be no African artistic renaissance without a corresponding spiritual renaissance. This was explicitly recognised by a congress of Negro writers who met in Rome in March 1959. A statement of theological beliefs was issued, signed by a Catholic, a Protestant, a Moslem and an Animist. It is worth quoting at length for it bears directly on our present subject.

Assumptions. We Africans who are believers, representatives of each faith, met together in theological subcommission assume:

1. that a difficult and grave responsibility rests on us in the present crisis of human values. A difficult responsibility, as religion entails the satisfaction of man's most absorbing needs, the rewards being neither material nor immediate. A grave responsibility, since the originality of our Negro-African culture is imperilled should the profoundly religious spirit that inspires it be extinguished;
2. that we have our own cultural heritage, the source of our originality;
3. that the fundamental values of this cultural heritage, which permit a valid dialogue between the various confessions in which the Black World lives, can be reduced to the following: a fundamental belief in a transcendent force, from which man derives his origins, on which he depends, to which he aspires; a sense of a vital solidarity, a term that seems to us the least removed from the Neddaku of the Peuhl, from the Maya of the Bamara, from the Fihavanana of the Malagash, etc., and thus contains the sum of moral and social virtues, such as the cult of ancestor worship, veneration of the elders, hospitality, the spirit of tolerance, etc.; a vital union between the spiritual and practical life;
4. that these fundamental values, by means of which the

80. Picasso: 'Danseur'. Oil. Paris, 1907. 5 ft. × 3 ft. 4 ins.

81. Picasso: Sculpture in painted wood.
Paris, 1907.

82. Brancusi: 'The Prodigal Son'. Sculpture in wood.
Height 2 ft. 6 ins. approx.

83. Modigliani: Limestone head, 1912. Height 1 ft. 11 ins.

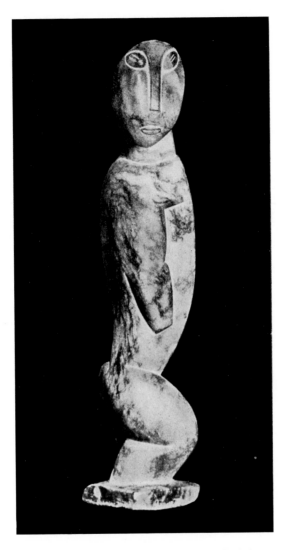

84. Gaudier-Brzeska: 'The Imp'. Veined alabaster,
1914. Height 1 ft. 4 ins.

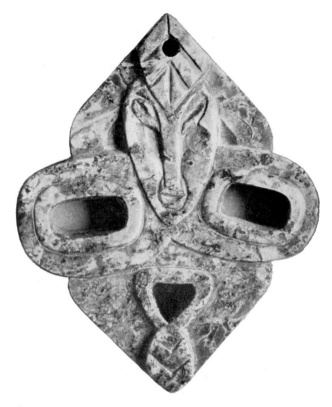

85. Gaudier-Brzeska: 'Amulet'. Green marble. Height 4 ins.
Width $3\frac{1}{2}$ ins.

86. K. Schmidt-Rottluff: Head in wood.

87. Wadiri, S. Nigeria. 'Jazz Scene'. 2 ft. × 1 ft. 6 ins.
London, 1958.

religious spirit of Africa is expressed, are suffering a two-fold crisis as a result of their encounter with the modern world and with foreign religions.

We declare:

1. that we must know our own cultural patrimony better and make it better known, profoundly permeated as it is by the religious spirit;

2. that we must make a clear assessment of what is decadent and what, on the contrary, is permanent in the manifestations of our cultural heritage;

3. that without prejudice we must welcome what is universal in any culture or religious manifestation, distinguishing the values in it that are universal (and, as a result, valid for all men) from those that are the expression of a specific cultural heritage;

4. that we mean to establish a dialogue between the different religions that animate the Negro-African world, a dialogue that will not produce an irreconcilable opposition between one religion and another but will appear as a mutually enriching gesture enabling each of them to find fulfilment in the context of Negro-African culture.

In my opinion the future of African art is to be found in this document. The key problem of the survival of an indigenous Negro-African culture is here squarely faced. We are a long way from the puerilities of the *ateliers*, such as have been recently opened at Brazzaville and elsewhere on the Black Continent, in which European artists instruct Africans in Western methods so that they may learn to produce the hybrid Afro-European 'pieces' which the market demands.

A spiritual sense, united to a thoroughgoing historical revaluation, is needed to eradicate the African's sense of inferiority. These two elements in conjunction could produce a dynamism sufficiently intense to rekindle the sacred fire in the descendants of the ancient artists. A new discharge of energy must vitalise the individual circuits before

M   *157*

the forces, at present quiescent, can be provoked into active life.

This does not mean that future African art must be exclusively religious. But it does mean that it is essential for the African artist to re-establish a vitally-felt bond with his traditional past. More than this, he must also make his own that psychological exaltation that derives from self-assertion in the face of adversity. When this happens, his works will cease to be merely worn-out repetitions of themes deeply alien to his sensibility, and will once again be invested with an interior strength.

The holy images that have been produced during the colonial period are artistically indifferent. The bronze crucifixes of the sixteenth and seventeenth centuries, produced in the Lower Congo, are much the same as present-day productions. The artist has achieved a syncretic blend of the old with the new. The brass candelabras cast for the Baule churches draw their inspiration directly from the pagan masks. Much of the work is pleasant enough, and reasonably accomplished in technique; but the power and grandeur of the old work is totally lacking. The pagan statuary had thaumaturgic powers. It could slay or heal from a distance. It could communicate with the kingdom of the dead, or become the seat of potent spirits. It was an object of fear and veneration.

There are no thaumaturgic properties to be found in the images of the new religion. On the contrary, they are clear evidence of a faith not yet fully assimilated. What would happen, for instance, were such holy images, sculpted by African hands, to be attended by the miraculous manifestations which have been connected with corresponding images in the West, such as weeping or sweating blood? It is difficult to envisage the events which might be set in motion. Perhaps a new art, the handmaid of a new religion, would arise—even if at the risk of re-enacting what happened at the end of the last century when—as Tata Nsiese relates—'the Christs and the statues became fetishes'.

But there is an obverse to Tata Nsiese's observation. It

is contained in two lines by Guillaume Apollinaire, and since 'idols' and 'fetishes' have occupied so much of our attention in the foregoing pages—even though they are spoken of to-day as in their twilight—it might not be out of place to conclude with this description of them:

Ils sont des Christs d'une autre foi et d'une autre croyance,
Ce sont les Christs inférieurs des obscures espérances.

BIBLIOGRAPHY

PREHISTORY, THE ROCK WORKS

ALIMEN, H., 'La station rupestre de Marhouma', *Mémoires de L'Institut de Recherches sahariennes*, Algiers, 1, 1954.

ALIMEN, H., *Préhistoire de l'Afrique*, Paris, 1955. English Edition, London, 1958.

ARAMBOURG, C., BOULE, M., VALLOIS, H., VERNEAU, R., 'Les grottes paléolithiques de Béni-Ségoual', letters *Archives de l'Institut de Paléontologie humaine, Mémoire*, 13, Paris, 1934.

BALOUT, L. and BRIGGS, L. C., 'Mechta el Arbi'. *Musée du Bardo*, iii-iv, Algiers, 1951.

BATTISS, W., *The Artists of the Rocks*, Pretoria, 1948.

BAUMANN, H., Vorläufiger Bericht über neue Felsbilder-Funde in Süd Angola', *Paideuma*, 6, Wiesbaden, 1954.

BLEEK, W. H. I. and LLOYD, L.C., *Das Wahre Gesicht des Buschmannes in seinen Mythen und Marchen*, Basel, 1938.

BOULE, M. and VALLOIS, H. V., 'L'homme fossile d'Asselar, Sahara', *Archives de Institut Paléontologie humaine, Mémoire*, 9, Paris, 1932.

BOULE, M. and VALLOIS, H.V., *Les Hommes Fossiles*, Paris, 1952.

BREUIL, H. and KEMAL EL DIN, 'Les gravures rupestres du Djebel Ouennat', in *Revue scientifique*, Paris, 1928.

BREUIL, H., 'L'Afrique préhistorique, *Cahiers d'Art*, 5, 1930, 8-9.

BREUIL, H., 'Peintures rupestres préhistoriques du Harrar (Abyssinie)', *L'Anthropologie*, vol. 44, 1934.

BREUIL, H., 'South African races in rock paintings', *Robert Broom Commemorative Volume, Royal Society of South Africa*, 1948.

BREUIL, H., 'The White Lady of Brandberg, South West Africa. Her Companions and her Guards', in *South African Archaeological Bulletin*, vol. 3, 1948.

BREUIL, H., 'Les roches peintes de l'Afrique australe et leur âge', in *L'Anthropologie*, vol. 53, 1949.

BREUIL, H. 'Les figures incisées et ponctuées de la grotte de Kiantapo (Katanga)', *Annales Musée royale de Congo Belge*, V. 1., Brussels, 1952.

Bibliography

BREUIL, H., 'Carbon Test and South-West African Paintings', in *South African Archaeological Bulletin*, 9 (no. 34).

BREUIL, H., 'Les roches peintes du Tasili-n-Ajjer', *A.M.G.*, Paris, 1954.

BREUIL, H. 'The White Lady of Brandberg', *Rock Paintings of Southern Africa*, London, 1955.

BRODRICK, A. H., *Prehistoric Painting*, London, 1948.

BROOM, R., 'The Boskop Skull', *Anthropological Papers of the American Museum of Natural History*, 23, New York, 1918.

BROOM, R. and SCHEPERS, G. W. H., *The South African fossil Ape-Men, the Australopithecinae*, Pretoria, 1946.

BURKITT, M., *South Africa's Past in Stone and Paint*, Cambridge, 1928.

CAPORIACCO (di), L. and GRAZIOSI, P., *Le pitture rupestri di Ain-Doua* (El Auenàt), Centro di Studi Coloniali, Florence, 1934.

CARVALHA (da), P., 'Rock Paintings at Mount Chimbamapere, Serra Vumba, Macequece', *Proceedings of the First Panafrican Congress of Prehistory*, 1947.

CHASSELOUP-LAURAT (de), F., *Art rupestre au Hoggar (Haut Mertoutek)*, Paris, 1938.

CLARK, J. D., *The Stone Age cultures of Northern Rhodesia*, published by the South African Archaeological Association, no. 1, Claremont, 1950.

COLE, S., *The Prehistory of East Africa*, Penguin Books, 1954.

DALLONI, M., *Géologie et préhistoire. Mission scientifique du Fezzan*. Institut de récherches sahariennes de l'Université d'Alger, 6, 1948.

DALLONI, M., 'Mission au Tibesti (1930-1931)', in *Mémoires de l'Académie des Sciences de l'Institut de France*, 62, Paris, 1935.

DARK, P. J. C., *Bush Negro Art*, London, 1954.

FLAMAND, G. B. M., *Les pierres écrites (Hadjrat-Mektoubat:) gravures et inscriptions rupestres du Nord-Africain*, Paris, 1921.

FROBENIUS, L. and OBERMAIER, H., *Hadschra Maktuba, Urzeitliche Felsbilder Kleinafrikas*, Munich, 1925.

FROBENIUS, L., *Madsimu Dsangara. Sudafrikanische Felsbilderchronik*, 2 vols., Berlin-Zürich, 1941.

FROBENIUS, L., *Ekade Ektab. Die Felsbilder Fezzans*, Leipzig, 1937.

FROBENIUS, L. and FOX, D.C., *Prehistoric Rock Pictures in Europe and Africa*, 1936. The Museum of Modern Art, New York, 1937.

Bibliography

GAUTIER, E. F., *Contribution à l'étude des gravures rupestres et inscriptions tifinar du Sahara Central*. Algiers, 1931.

GRAZIOSI, P., *L'Arte rupestri della Libia*, 2 vols., Naples, 1942.

HUARD, P., 'Etat des recherches au Tchad', *Extrait des Tropiques*, 1952-53.

HUARD, P., 'Gravures rupestres des confins Nigéro-Tchadiens', *Bulletin de l'Institut Français Afrique Noire*, Dakar, October, 1953.

IACOVLEFF, A., *Dessins et peintures d'Afrique*, 1927.

JOHNSON, J. P., *The Prehistoric Period in South Africa*, London, 1910.

JONES, N., *The Stone Age in Rhodesia*, London, 1926.

JONES, N., 'The Prehistory of Southern Rhodesia', *Museum Memoir*, 2, Cambridge, 1949.

LEAKEY, L. S. B., *The Stone Age cultures of Kenya Colony*, Cambridge, 1931.

LEAKEY, M. and L., *Excavations at the Njoro River Cave*, Oxford, 1950.

LEAKEY, L. S. B., 'Prehistoric Art in Tanganyika', *Actes du IIe Congrés panafricain de préhistoire*, Algiers, 1952.

LEAKEY, L. S. B., *Adam's Ancestors*, London, 1954.

LELUBRE, M., 'Contribution à la préhistoire au Sahara. Les peintures du Dohone (Tibesti Nord-Oriental)', *Bulletin de la Société préhistorique Française*, Vol. xlv, 1948.

LHOTE, H., 'Les peintures rupestres de Tit (Ahaggar)', *L'Anthropologie*, 58, Paris, 1954.

MONOD, T., 'L'Adrar Ahnet, Contribution à l'étude archéologique d'un district saharien', *Travaux et Mémoires de l'Institut de Ethnologie*, 19, Paris, 1932.

MONOD, T., 'Contribution à l'étude du Sahara occid.', *Bulletin du Comité d'Etudes historiques et scientifiques de l'A.O.F.*, series A, no. 7, Dakar, 1938.

MORI, F., 'Ricerche paleontologiche nel Fezzan', *Rivista di Scienze Preistoriche*, vol. xi, Nos. 1-4, Florence, 1956.

MORI, F., 'Nuove scoperte d'arte rupestre nell'Acacus (Fezzan), *Rivista di Scienze Preistoriche*, vol. xii, Nos. 3-4, Florence, 1957.

MORTELMANS, G., 'Les dessins rupestres gravés, ponctués et peints du Katanga, Essai de synthèse', *Annales du Musée royale du Congo Belge*, V. 1, Tervueren, 1952.

MOSZEIK, O., *Die Malereien der Buschmänner in Südafrika*, Berlin, 1910.

Bibliography

MURRAY, G. W. and MYERS, O. H., 'Some Pre-dynastic Rock Drawings', *Journal of Egyptian Archaeology*, xix, 1933.

NEWBOLD, D., 'Rock-pictures and Archaeology in the Libyan Desert', *Antiquity*, September 1928, pp. 261-91.

OBERMAIER, H. and KUHN, H., *Bushman Art. Rock Paintings of South-West Africa*, London, 1930.

REYGASSE, M., 'La préhistoire du Sahara Central (Hoggàr et Tassili des Ajjers)', *Congrès Préhistorique de France*, 11th session, 1934.

REYGASSE, M., 'Gravures et peintures rupestres du Tassili des Ajjers', *L'Anthropologie*, vol. 45, 1935.

RIET LOWE (van) C., 'Rock paintings in Northern Rhodesia', *South African Journal of Sciences*, vol. xxxiv, 1937.

RIET LOWE (van), C., 'L'âge et l'origine des peintures rupestres d'Afrique', *L'Anthropologie*, vol. 54, 1950.

RIET LOWE (van), C. 'A Note on Prehistoric Classification', *Man*, 122, London, 1954.

SANDFORD, H. S. and ARKELL, A. J., 'Paleolithic Man and the Nile-Faiyum Divide', *University of Chicago Oriental Institute Publications*, vol. 17, Chicago, 1929.

SANTOS, (dos), F., 'On the prehistory of Mozambique', *Moçambique*, no. 28, 1941.

SCHOFIELD, J. F., 'L'art et les auteurs des rupestres d'Afrique australe', *L'Anthropologie*, vol. 55, Paris, 1951.

SCHOFIELD, J. F., 'L'âge des peintures rupestres de l'Afrique du Sud, *L'Anthropologie*, vol. 53, Paris, 1949.

SCHWEINFURTH, G., 'Über alte Tierbilder und Felsinschriften bei Assuan', *Zeitschrift für Ethnologie*, Berlin, vol. 44, 1912.

SOLIGNAC, M., *Les pierres écrites de la Berbérie Orientale*, Tunis, 1928.

SUMMERS, R., 'A Tentative Correlation of Southern African Stone Age Cultures', *University of London Institute of Archaeology, Annual Report*, 9, London, 1953.

TONGUE, H., *Bushman Paintings*, London, 1909.

VALLOIS, H. V., 'L'homme fossile de Rabat', *Compt. rend. Académie Science*, Vol. 221, Paris, 1945.

VALLOIS, H. V., 'La mandibule . . . de Diré-Daoua', *L'Anthropologie*, vol. 55, Paris, 1951.

VAUFREY, R., 'L'Art rupestre Nord-Africain', *Archives de L'Institut de Paléontologie humaine*, Mémoire, 20, Paris, 1939.

Bibliography

WILLCOX, A. R., 'The Shaded Polychrome Paintings of South Africa, their Distribution, Origin and Age', *South African Archaeological Association Bulletin*, 10, Claremont, 1955.

WILMANN, M., 'The Rock Engravings of Griqualand West and Bechuanaland, South Africa', Cambridge, Kimberley, *Alex. McGregor Memorial Museum*, 1933.

WINKLER, H. A., *Völker u. Völkerbewegungen im vorgeschichtlichen Oberägypten im Lichte neuer Felsbilderfunde*, Stuttgart, 1937.

WINKLER, H. A., *Rock Drawings of Southern Upper Egypt*, London, 1938-39.

ZELTNER (de), F., 'Grottes à peintures du Soudan français', *L'Anthropologie*, vol. 22, 1911.

ZELTNER (de), F., 'Les gravures rupestres de l'Aïr', *L'Anthropologie*, vol. 24, 1913.

ZOLI, C., 'Le sculpture rupestri del Fezzan', *Rivista delle Colonie italiane*, Rome, 1928.

HISTORY, ETHNOGRAPY, ARCHAEOLOGY

AFRICANUS, LEO (Hassan ibn Mohammed el-Uzzan, 1492-1525), *Africae Descriptio*, Amsterdam, 1632. English edn. (John Pory), London, 1895.

ADEREM (Oni di Ifé), 'Notes on the City of Ifé', *Nigeria*, no. 12, Lagos, 1937.

ALBERICH, J. C., 'Problemas de contacto de culturas en Africa', *Cuadernos Africanos y Orientales*, 30, Madrid, 1955.

ANKERMANN, B., *Totenkult und Seelenglauben bei den afrikanischen Völkern*, 1918.

ARKELL, A. J., *A History of the Sudan to A.D. 1821*, London, 1955.

ARMATTOE, E. E. G., *The Golden Age of West African Civilization*, Londonderry, 1946.

ASHTON, HUGH, *The Basuto*, London, New York, Toronto, 1952.

BACON, R. H. S., *Benin, the city of blood*, London-New York, 1897.

BARTH, H., *Reisen und Entdeckungen in Nord und Central Africa*, Gotha, 1857.

BAUMANN, O., *Durch Massailand zur Nilquelle*, Berlin, 1894.

BAXTER, P. T. W. and BUTT, A., 'The Azande and Related

Bibliography

Peoples of the Anglo-Egyptian Sudan and Belgian Congo', *Ethnographic Survey of Africa: East Central Africa*, 9, London, 1953.

BAUMANN, N., 'Benin', *Cahiers d'Art*, nos. 3-5, Paris, 1930.

BAUMANN, H., *Schöpfung und Urzeit des Menschen im Mythus der Afrikanischen Völker*, Berlin, 1936.

BAUMANN, H., 'Steingräber und Steinbauten in Angola', *Beiträge zur Kolonialforschung*, Bd. 1, Berlin, 1943.

BAUMANN, H. and WESTERMAN, D., *Les Peuples et les civilizations de l'Afrique*, Paris, 1948.

BAUMANN, H., 'Die Frage der Steinbauten und Steingräber in Angola', *Paideuma*, vi Bd., 1956.

BEAUCORPS (de), R., *Les Basongo de la Luniungu et de la Gobari*, Brussels, 1941.

BEAUVAIS PALISOT (de), 'Notice sur le Peuple de Benin', *Décade Philosophique*, Année, 9, no. 12, 1801.

BEECHAM, J., *Ashantee and the Gold Coast*, London, 1841.

BEIER, U., 'The Palace of the Ogogas in Ikerre', *Nigeria*, no. 44, Lagos, 1954.

BENEZET, A., *Some historical account of Guinea*, Philadelphia, 1771.

BENT, J. T., *The Ruined Cities of Mashonaland*, 1893.

BERTHELOT, A., *L'Afrique saharienne et soudanaise, ce qu'en ont connu les anciens*, Paris, 1927.

BERTHO, J. and MAUNY, R., 'Archéologie du Pays Yoruba et du Bas-Niger', *Notes Africaines*, no. 56, Ifan, Dakar, 1952.

BITTREMIEUX, L., *La Société Secrète des Bakhimba au Mayombe*, Brussels, 1936.

BITTREMIEUX, L., *De Inwijking der Baphende Congo*, 1938.

BLAKE, J. W., *Europeans in West Africa, 1450-1560*, London, 1942.

BLONDEL, C., *La Mentalité primitive*, Paris, 1926.

BOEUF, Y. F., 'Etudes sur les Bozo du Niger occidental', *Outre-Mer*, no. 4, Paris, 1934.

BOISRAGON (Capt.), A., *The Benin Massacre*, London, 1897.

BOSH (Van den), R. P., 'Quelques notes sur le nom et la notion de l'Etre Suprême chez les Balendu', *Anthropos*, 23, St Gabriel-Mödling, 1928.

BOSMAN, W., *Description de la Guinée*, Utrecht, 1704.

BOUISSON, M., *La Magie*, Paris, 1958.

Bibliography

BOULNOIS, J. and HAMA BOUBOU, *L'Empire de Gao. Histoire, Coutumes et Magie des Sonrai*, Paris, 1954.

BOVILL, E. W., *Caravans of the Sahara: An Introduction to the History of Western Sudan*, Oxford, 1933.

BOWDICH, T. E., *Mission from Cape Coast Castle to Ashantee*, London, 1819.

BRÉVIÉ, *L'Islamisme contre Naturisme*, Paris, 1923.

BRUNNER, S., *Reise nach Senegambien*, Berne, 1840.

BRYK, F., *Dark Rapture. The Sex Life of the African Negro*, New York, 1939.

BURNIER, T., *Ames primitives. Contribution à l'étude du sentiment religieux chez les païens animistes*, Paris, 1922.

BURTON, F. R., *A Mission to Gelele, King of Dahome*, London, 1864.

CA DA MOSTO (de), A., *Relation des voyages à la Côte Occidentale d'Afrique*, Ed. Schefer, Paris, 1895.

CAILLIÉ, R., *Travels through Central Africa to Timbuctoo and across the Great Desert to Morocco*, London, 1830.

CARETTE, E., *Recherches sur l'origine et les migrations des principales tribus de l'Afrique Septentrionale*, Paris, 1853.

CARLI, D., *Il Moro trasportato in Venezia*, Reggio, 1672.

CATON THOMPSON, G., *The Zimbabwe Culture*, Oxford, 1931.

CAVAZZI DA MONTECUCCOLA, G. A., *Historica descrizione dei tre regni Congo, Matamba et Angola, situati nell'Etiopia inferiore occidentale*, Bologna, 1687.

CECCHI, A., *Da Zeila alle frontiere del Caffa*, Rome, 1885-87.

CHARDEY, F., 'Résurrection d'un mort et apparition des morts chez les Ewe', *Anthropos*, XLVI, Freiburg, 1951.

CHÉRON, G., 'Les Minianka. Leur civilisation matérielle', *Revue d'Ethnologie et de Sociologie*, 1913.

CHÉRON, G., 'Les Bobo Fing', *Bulletin du Comité d'études historiques et scientifiques de l'A.O.F.*, Paris, 1916.

COLLE, R. P., *Les Baluba*, Brussels, 1913.

COMHAIRE, J., 'Sociétés secrètes et mouvements prophétiques au Congo Belge', *Africa*, 25, London, 1955.

CORDERO DI MONTEZEMOLO, B., 'Le armi congolesi . . .' *Riv. di Antropologia*, xxii, 1938-39.

CORSO, R., *Studi Africani*, Naples, 1950.

COTTON, E. P., 'The Mind of Primitive Man in West Africa', *Journal of Applied Sociology*, vol. ix, Los Angeles, 1924.

COURDIOUX, P. E., *La Côte des Esclaves*, Paris, 1924.

Bibliography

CRAWFORD, O. G. S., *The Fung Kingdom of Sennar*, Gloucester, 1951.

CRAZZALARA, J. P., *The Lwoo, Lwoo Traditions*, Museum Combonianum, Verona, 1951.

CRONE, G. R.,*The Voyages of Cadamosto and other documents on Western Africa in the second half of the Fifteenth Century*, London, 1937.

CRUZ (da), C., 'Les instruments de musique dans le Bas-Dahomey', *Études Dahoméennes*, 12, Dahomey, 1954.

CUNARD, N. (editress), *Negro Anthology*, contains many papers by various authors. London, 1934.

CUREAU, A., *Les Sociétés Primitives de l'Afrique Equatoriale*, Paris 1912. *Savage Man in Central Africa*, English edition, London, 1915.

CUVELIER, J. and JADIN, L., *L'Ancien Congo d'après les archives romaines (1518-1640)*, Brussels, 1954.

DALZEL, A., *History of Dahomey*, London, 1793.

DAMMANN, E., *Beiträge aus arabischen Quellen zur Kenntnis des negerischen Afrika*, Kiel, 1929.

DANZEL, T. W., *Magie et Science Secrète*, Paris, 1947.

DAPPER, O., *Description de l'Afrique*, Amsterdam, 1686.

DAVIDSON, J., 'La Circoncision chez les Ngombe', *Aequatoria*, Coquilhatville, 14, 1951.

DELAFOSSE, M., 'Le Peuple Siena ou Senoufo', *Revue des études ethnographique et Sociologique*, Paris, 1908-9.

DELAFOSSE, M., *Haut-Sénégal Niger*, 3 vols., Paris, 1912.

DELAFOSSE, M., *Civilizations Negro-Africaines*, Paris, 1925.

DELAFOSSE, M., *Les Nègres*, Paris, 1927.

DELHAISE (Com), *Les Warega*, Brussels, 1909.

DELOBSON, D., *L'Empire du Mogho Naba*, Paris, 1932.

DELOBSON, D., 'Les Danses Mossi et leur signification', *Revue Anthropologique*, vol. 13, Paris, 1932.

DE MARTINO, E., *Il mondo magico*, Turin, 1948.

DENHAM, D. and CLAPPERTON, H., *Narrative of Travels and Discoveries in Northern and Central Africa*, London, 1826.

DENNETT, R. E., *At the Back of the Black Man's Mind*, London, 1906.

DENNETT, R. E., *Nigerian Studies*, London, 1910.

DENTI DI PIRAJNO, A., *Incantesimi neri*, Milan, 1959.

DE QUATTINI, M. and CARLI, D., *Viaggio nel Regno di Congo*, Rome, 1648.

Bibliography

DESCHAMPS, H., *Les Antaisaka. Géographie humaine, histoire et coutumes d'une population malgache*, Tananarive, 1938.

DIER, P. M., *Unter den Schwarzen*, Steyl, 1899.

DIETERLEN, G., *Les âmes des Dogon*, Paris, 1941.

DIETERLEN, G., *La Religion Bambara*, Paris, 1951.

DOKE, C. M., 'The Basis of Bantu Literature', *Africa*, London, October, 1948.

DUGAST, I., 'Monographie de la tribu de Ndiki', *Travaux et Mémoires de L'Institut d'Ethnologie*, 58 and 63, Paris, 1955.

EDRISI (Abu 'Abdallah Muhammad ben Muhammad al, born 1100), *Description de l'Afrique et de l'Espagne*. Translated by E. Dozy and M. J. de Goeje, Leyde, 1866.

EGHAREVBA, H. U., *A Short History of Benin*, Lagos, 1936.

ELLIS, A. B., *History of the Gold Coast of West Africa*, London, 1893.

ELLIS, A. B., *Yoruba-Speaking Peoples*, London, 1894.

ELLIS, A. B., *The Tshi-speaking Peoples of the Gold Coast of West Africa*, London, 1887.

ENGERSTRÖM, T., *Apport à la théorie des origines du peuple et de la langue Peuhle*, Stockholm, 1954.

FALCONER, T., *Voyage of Hanno translated and accompanied with the Greek text*, London, 1797.

FARROW, S. S., *Faith, Fancies and Fetich*, London, 1926.

FEUILLOLEY, B. F., 'Magic and Initiation in the Ubanghi-Shari', *Negro Anthology*, ed. N. Cunard, London, 1934.

FONTAINE, P., *La Magie chez les Noirs*, Paris, 1949.

FORBES, F., *Dahomey and the Dahomans*, London, 1851.

FORDE, D. and JONES, G. I., 'The Ibo and Ibibio-Speaking Peoples of South-Eastern Nigeria, *Ethnographic Survey of Africa: Western Africa*, 3, London, 1950.

FORDE, D., 'The Yoruba-Speaking Peoples of South-Western Nigeria', *Ethnographic Survey of Africa: Western Africa*, vols. 1-12.

FRAZER, J. G., *The Golden Bough*, London, 1907.

FRANKFORT, H., 'The African Foundation of Ancient Egyptian Civilization', *Atti I Congr. Int. Preist. e Protost. Mediterr.*, Florence, 1950.

FROBENIUS, L., *Der schwarze Dekameron, Liebe, Witz und Heldentum in Inner-Afrika*, Berlin-Charlottenburg, 1910.

FROBENIUS, L., *Schwarze Seelen. Afrikanisches Tag- und Nachtlehen*, Berlin-Charlottenburg, 1913.

Bibliography

FROBENIUS, L., *Atlantis. Völksmärchen und Volksdichtungen Afrikas.* 12 vols., Jena, 1912-28.

FROBENIUS, L., *Atlas Africanus.* Belege zur Morphologie der afrikanischen Kulturen, 12 parti, 49 fascic., Munich-Berlin, 1922-30.

FROBENIUS, L., *Das unbekannte Afrika. Aufhellung der Schicksale eines Erdteils,* Munich, 1923.

FROBENIUS, L., *Märchen aus Kordofan,* Jena, 1923.

FROBENIUS, L., *Erlebte Erdteile. Ergebnisse deutschen Forscherlebens,* 7 vols., Frankfurt-on-Main, 1925-30.

FROBENIUS, L., 'Afrikanischer Tanz', *Rheinisch-Westfälische Zeitung,* Essen, 8 August 1928.

FROBENIUS, L. and BREUIL, H., 'Afrique', *Cahiers d'Art,* Paris, 1931.

FROBENIUS, J. *Erithräa, Länder und Zeiten des heiligen Königsmordes,* Berlin-Zürich, 1931.

FROBENIUS, L., 'Mensch und Maske', *Der Erdball,* 6, 1932.

FROBENIUS, L., *'Kulturgeschichte Afrikas. Prolegomena zu einer historischen Gestaltlehre,* Zürich, 1933. Italian edition. *Storia della Civiltà Africana,* Turin, 1950.

FROBENIUS, L. and FOX, D., *African Genesis,* New York, 1937: *The Voice of Africa,* 2 vols., London, 1913.

FROBENIUS, L., 'Die Waremba, Träger einer fossilen Kultur', *Zeitschrift für Ethnologie,* 70, Brunswick, 1922.

FUHRMANN, E., *Afrika,* Munich, 1922.

GAMITTON, O., *Muata Cazembe,* Lisbon, 1854.

GARBUTT, H. W., 'Native Superstitions and Witchcraft in South Africa', *Journal of the Royal Anthropological Institute,* 39, London, 1939.

GARCIA, 'Moeurs et coutumes des Teda du Tou', *Bulletin de l'Institut des études Centralafricaines,* no. 10, Paris, 1955.

GENNEP (Van), A., *Les rites de passage,* Paris, 1909.

GENNEP (Van), A., *L'étude actuelle du problème totémique,* Paris, 1920.

GIGLIARELLI, U., *Il Fezzan,* Tripoli, 1932.

GIOIA DA NAPLES, F. M., *Conversione della Regina Singa e del suo regno di Matamba,* Naples, 1669.

GLÜCK, J. F., 'Afrikanische Architektur', *Tribus,* Band 6, Stuttgart, 1957.

GLUCKMAN, M., 'Circumcision Rites of the Balovale Tribes', *African Studies,* 13, Johannesburg, 1954.

Bibliography

GODEFROY LOYER (Père), *Relation du voyage du royaume d'Issyny*, Paris, 1714.

GORDON, P., *Initiation sexuelle et évolution religieuse*, Paris, 1946.

GORER, G., *Africa Dances*, London, 1935.

GRAFT-JOHNSON (de), J. C., *African Glory. The Story of Vanished Negro Civilizations*, London, 1954. Italian edition, Feltrinelli, Milan, 1957.

GREBERT, F., *Au Gabun*, Paris, 1948.

GRIAULE, M., 'Le Mythe de l'organisation du monde chez les Dogon du Soudan', *Psyché*, nos. 13-14, November-December 1947.

GRIAULE, M., *Dieu d'eau*, Paris, 1948.

GRIAULE, M., *Folk Art of Black Africa*, New York, 1950.

GROS, J., *Voyages, Aventures et Captivite de Bonnat chez les Ashantis*, Paris, 1884.

HALL, H. U., *Some Gods of the Yoruba*, Philadelphia, 1917.

HALL, H. U., *The Sherbro of Sierra Leone*, Philadelphia, 1938.

HALL, R. N., *The Ancient Ruins of Rhodesia*, London, 1904.

HARDY, G., *Vue Générale de l'Histoire d'Afrique*, Paris, 1948.

HARLEY, G. W., *Notes on the Poro in Liberia*, Cambridge, Mass., 1941.

HARLEY, G. W., *Masks as Agents of Social Control in Northeast Liberia*, Cambridge, Mass., 1941.

HARPER, 'Notes on the Totemism of the Gold Coast', *Journal of Anthropology*, no. 36, London, 1906.

HARRISON, J. E. *Ancient Art and Ritual*, New York, 1913-48.

HAY, J., *Ashanti and the Gold Coast and what we know of it*, London, 1874.

HEEREN, A. H. L., *African Nations*, Oxford, 1832.

HENRY (Abbé), J., 'L'Ame d'un peuple africain. Les Bambara: leur vie psychique, éthique sociale-religieuse, Bibl. *Anthropos*, Münster, 1910.

HERSKOVITZ, M. J., *Dahomey*, 2 vols., New York, 1938.

HESS, J., *L'Ame Nègre*, Paris, 1899.

HILLS, Y. E., *Female Circumcision in the Sudan*, London, 1949.

HIRSCHBERG, W., 'Kultureinflüsse Meroes und Napatas auf Negerafrika', *Wiener Völkerkundl. Mitteil.*, 3, Vienna, 1955.

HUBBARD, J. W., *The Sobo of the Niger Delta*, Zaria (Nigeria), 1948.

Bibliography

HUBER, H., 'Semaine Internationale d'études sur la formation religieuse et humaine en Afrique Noire', *Anthropos*, vol. 50, Freiburg, 1955.

HUGGINS, W. N. and JACKSON, J. G., *An Introduction to African Civilization*, New York, 1937.

HUNTINGFORD, G. W. B., 'Egypt in Africa', *Ancient Egypt*, 1925, Part iv.

IBN BATUTA ('Abullah ibn Muhammad, born 1304), *Travels in Asia and Africa*, selected and translated by H. A. R. Gibb, London, 1929.

IBN BATUTA ('Abdallah ibn Muhammad, born 1304), *Voyages*, translated by C. Defremery and B. R. Sanguinetti, 4 vols., Paris, 1858, 1922.

IBN KHALDUN (Abu Zakarya Yahya, born 1332), *Prolégomènes Historiques*, translated by De Slane, Paris, 1865.

IDRISSOU MBOROU N'JOYA, 'Le Sultanat du pays Bamoun et son origine', *Bulletin de la Société d'Etudes Cameroun.* no. 7, December, 1935.

JEFFREYS, M. D. W., 'The Cowry Shell: A study of its history and use in Nigeria', *Nigeria*, Lagos, September, 1938.

JEFFREYS, M. D. W., 'Le Serpent a deux têtes Bamoun', *Bulletin de la Société d'études Cameroun*, no. 9, March, 1945.

JEFFREYS, M. D. W., 'Circumcision: Its Diffusion from Egypt among the Bantu', *Criteria*, I, March, 1949.

JENSEN, A. E., *Mythes et cultes chez les peuples primitifs*, Paris, 1954.

JOSET, P. E., 'Notes ethnographiques sur la sous-tribu des Walese-Abfunkotou', *Bulletin des Jurisdictions Indigènes*, Elisabethville, January-June, 1949.

KAGAME, A., *La Poésie Dynastique au Rwanda*, Brussels, 1951.

KAGAME, A., *Les organisations socio-familiares de l'ancien Rwanda*, Brussels, 1954.

KAIGH, F., *Witchcraft and Magic in Africa*, London, 1947.

KATI MAHMOUD (ben el-Hadj el Molauakkil Kati), *Tarikh el-Fettach*, translated by Houdas and Delafosse, Paris, 1913.

KEIMER, L., 'Notes prisés chez les Bišarīn et les Nubiens d'Assuan, *Bulletin de L'Institut d'Egypte*, xxxii, 1951; xxxiii, 1952, xxxiv, 1953; xxxv, 1954.

KEIMER, L., 'Egypt in Africa', *Egypt Travel Magazine*, no. 28, November, 1956.

Bibliography

KENYATTA, J., *Facing Mount Kenya*, London, 1st ed. 1938. (Italian translation in the 'Avanti' series, 1954: 'I Kikuyu'.)

KERHARO, J. and BOUQUET, A., *Sorciers Féticheurs et Guérisseurs de la Côte d'Ivoire-Haute Volta*, Paris, 1950.

KINGSLEY, M., *Travels in West Africa*, London, 1897.

KINGSLEY, M., *West African Studies*, London, 1897.

LABOURET, M. H., 'Notes contributives à l'étude du peuple Baoule', *Revue d'Ethnographie et de Sociologie*, Paris, 1914.

LABOURET, M. H. and TRAVELE, M., 'Le Théâtre Mandingue', *Africa*, vol. i. London, 1928.

LABOURET, M. H., 'Les tribus du Rameau Lobi, *Travaux et Mémoires de l'Institut d'Ethnologie*, 15, Paris, 1931.

LABOURET, M. H., 'Les Manding et leur langue', *Bulletin du Comité d'études historiques et scientifiques de l'A.O.F.*, Paris, 1936.

LABOURET, M. H., *Histoire des Noirs d'Afrique*, Paris, 1950.

LAGERCRANTZ, S., 'Der Donnerkeil im afrikanischen Volksglauben, *Ethnologiska Studier*, no. 10, Gothenberg, 1940.

LAIRD, M. and OLDFIELD, R. A. K., *Expedition into the Interior of Africa by the River Niger*, London, 1837.

LAMAN, K., *The Kongo*, V.1, Upsala, 1953. V. 2, Upsala, 1957.

LATOUCHE, J., *Congo*, New York, 1945.

LAYCOCK, H. T., 'Surgical aspects of female circumcision in Somaliland', *East African Medical Journal*, November, 1950.

LAYDEVANT, P., 'L'enfance chez les Basuto', *Annali Lateranensi*, Rome, December, 1948.

LAYE CAMARA, *L'Enfant Noir*, Paris, 1954.

LAVIGOTTE, H., *L'Evur, croyance des Pahouins du Gabon*, Paris, 1947.

LEBEUF, J. P. and DETOURBET, A. M., *La Civilisation du Tchad*, Paris, 1950.

LE CHATELIER, A., *L'Islam dans l'Afrique occidentale*, Paris, 1899.

LECLANT, J., 'Egypte-Afrique, quelques remarques sur la diffusion des monuments égyptiens en Afrique', *Bulletin de la Société Française d'Egypt*, 21, 1956.

LEIRIS, M., 'Objets rituels Dogon. Masques Dogon. Danses funéraires Dogon', *Minotaure*, Paris, 1933.

Le Livre africain, Brussels, March, 1959. (Monthly Bulletin. Contains the new phonetic transcriptions of the names of the African tribes.)

N

173

Bibliography

LEM, F. H., 'Culte des arbres au Soudan', *Bulletin 10, l'Institut Français d'Afrique Noire*, Dakar, 1942.

LEM, F. H., 'Magie Soudanaise', *Soleil*: no. 1, Paris, 1947.

LENZ, O., *Timbuktu*, Leipzig, 1884. French translation, 2 vols., Paris, 1890.

LEONARD, A. G., *The Lower Niger and its Tribes*, London, 1906.

LE ROY, A., *La Religion des Primitifs*, Paris, 1911.

LÉVI-BRÜHL, L., *Les fonctions mentales dans les sociétés inférieures*, Paris, 1910.

LÉVI-BRÜHL, L., *La Mentalité prélogique*, Paris, 1922.

LÉVI-BRÜHL, L., *L'anima primitiva*, Turin, 1949.

LEWIS, I. M., 'Peoples of the Horn of Africa, Somali, Afar and Sabo', *Ethnographic Survey of Africa: North-Eastern Africa I, International African Institute*, London, 1955.

L'Habitat au Cameroun, Ed. l'Union Française, Paris, 1952.

LIETARD, L., 'Les Waregas', *Bulletin de la Société royale Belge de Géographie*, Brussels, 1923.

LINDSKOG, B., *African Leopard Man*, Upsala, 1954.

LUCAS, O., J., *The Religion of the Yorubas*, Lagos, 1948.

MCCULOGH, M., *Peoples of Sierra Leone Protectorate*, London, 1951.

MACDONALD, G., *Gold Coast Past and Present*, London, 1898.

MAES, J., *Notes sur les populations des Bassins du Kasai, de la Lukanie et du Lac Léopold II*, Brussels, 1924.

MAES, J. and BOONE, O., *Les Peuplades du Congo Belge*, Brussels, 1935.

MAISTRE, A., *A travers l'Afrique centrale*, Paris, 1895.

MALINOWSKI, B., *The Dynamics of Culture Change*, New Haven, 1946.

MALINOWSKI, B., *Magic, Science and Religion*, New York, 1948.

MALINOWSKI, B., *Sex and Repression in Savage Society*, New York, 1951.

MANOUKIAN, M., *Akan and Ga-Adangme Peoples of the Gold Coast*, London, 1950.

MARTY, P., *Etudes sur l'Islam et les tribus du Soudan*, Paris, 1920.

MATTHEWS, J., *Voyage to the River Sierra Leone*, London, 1788.

MAUNY, R., 'Où en est la toponymie Ouest-africaine', *Revue Internationale d'Onomastique*, 3, Paris, 1951.

MEROLLA DA SORRENTO, G., *Breve e succinta relazione del viaggio nel Regno di Congo nell'Africa meridionale*, Naples, 1692.

Bibliography

MEYEROWITZ, E., *Akan Traditions of Origin*, London, 1950.

MEYEROWITZ, E., 'Concepts of the Soul among the Akan of the Gold Coast', *Africa*, London, January, 1951.

MEYEROWITZ, E., *The Sacred State of Akan*, London, 1951.

MICHELET, R., ' "Primitive" Life and Mentality', *Negro*, ed. N. Cunard, London, 1934.

MICHELET, R., 'African Empires and Civilizations', *Negro*, ed. N. Cunard, London, 1934.

MOLLIEN, G., *Travels in the Interior of Africa to the Sources of the Senegal and Gambia*, London, 1820.

MOLLIEN, G., *Voyage dans l'intérieur de l'Afrique*, Paris, 1822.

MONTEIL, C., *Les Bambara du Segou et du Kaata*, Paris, 1924.

MORGEN, G., *Durch Kamerun von Süd nach Nord*, Leipzig, 1893.

MORIE, L. J., *Histoire de Nubie et d'Abyssinie*, Paris, 1904.

MORS, O., 'Geschichte der Bahinda des alten Kyamtwara-Reiches am Victoria-Nyanza-See', *Anthropos*, vol. 50, Freiburg, 1955.

MUNDAY, J. T., 'Spirit Names among the Central Bantu', *African Studies*, Johannesburg, March, 1948.

MURDOCK, G. P., *Our Primitive Contemporaries*, New York, 1934.

NADEL, S. F., *A Black Byzantium*, London, 1951.

NORRS, R., *Mémoires du Règne de Bossa-Ahadée, Roi de Dahomé*, Paris, 1790.

NYENDAEL (van), D., *Beschryving van Rio Formosa anders gesegt de Benin*, Amsterdam, 1709.

OLDEROGGE, D. and POTECHIN, I., *Narody Afriki*, Moscow, 1954.

PALMER, R., *The Bornu Sahara and Sudan*, London, 1936.

PARK, MUNGO, *Voyage dans l'intérieur de l'Afrique fait en 1795, 1796 et 1797*, 2 vols., Paris, 1799.

PARK, MUNGO, *Second Voyage dans l'intérieur de l'Afrique fait en 1805*, Paris, 1820. English edition, *Life and Travels*, Edinburgh, 1838.

PARRINDER, G., *La Religion en Afrique Occidentale*, Paris, 1950.

PARRINDER, G., *West African Psychology*, London, 1951.

PARRINDER, E. G., *African Traditional Religion*, London, 1954.

PAULME, D., *Organisation sociale des Dogon* (Soudan Français), Paris, 1940.

Bibliography

PAULME, D., 'L'Excision en Pays Kissi', *Comptes-Rendues sommaires des Scéanes de l'Institut Français d'Anthropologie*, Paris, 1947-49.

PAULME, D., *Les Civilisations Africaines*, Paris, 1953.

PEDRALS (de), D. P., *Manuel Scientifique de l'Afrique Noire*, Paris, 1949.

PEDRALS (de), D. P., *Archéologie de l'Afrique Noire*, Paris, 1950.

PETTERSSON, O., *Chiefs and Gods. Religious and Social Elements in the South Eastern Bantu Kingship*, Lund, 1953.

PIGAFETTA, F., *Relazione del Reame di Congo e delle Circonvicine Contrade tratta dalli scritti e ragionamenti di Odlordo Lopez*, Rome, 1501. 'A Report on the Kingdom of Congo. . . . 1591', translated by H. Hutchinson, London, 1881.

POOLE, T. E., *Life, Scenery and Customs in Sierra Leone*, London, 1850.

POSSOZ, E., 'L'onomastique en Afrique Noire', *Revue Internationale d'Onomastique*, Paris, 1950.

PROYART, L. B., *Histoire de Loango, Kakongo et autres royaumes d'Afrique*, Paris, 1776.

RADCLIFFE-BROWN, A. R. and FORDE, D., *African System of Kinship and Marriage*, London, 1950.

RATTRAY, R. S., *Religion and Art in Ashanti*, Oxford, 1960 (reprint).

REINDORF, C. C., *History of the Gold Coast and Ashantee*, Basle, 1895.

RICHARDS, AUDREY I., *Economic Development and Tribal Change*, Cambridge (no date).

RICHARD-MOLARD, J., *L'Afrique Occidentale Française*, Paris, 1949.

RITTER, E. A., *Shaka Zulu. The Rise of the Zulu Empire*, London, 1955.

RONCIÈRE (de la), C., *La découverte de l'Afrique au moyen âge*, 3 vols., Cairo, 1924-28.

ROSS, E., *African Heritage*, New York, 1952.

ROTH, H. LING, *Great Benin—Its Customs, Art and Horrors*, Halifax, 1903.

RYAN, I., *Black Man's Town*, London, 1953.

SÄVE-SÖDERBERGH, T., *Aegypten und Nubien*, Lund, 1941.

SCHEBESTA, P., 'Die Simbabwe-Kultur in Afrika', *Anthropos*, 21, 6 St Gabriel Mödling, 1926.

Bibliography

SCHIAPARELLI, E., *La Geografia dell'Africa Orientale secondo le indicazioni dei monumenti egiziani*, Accademia dei Lincei, Rome, 1916.

SCHMELTZ, J. V. E., 'Neue Litteratur über Benin', *Internationales Archiv für Ethnograpfiie*, Leiden, 1903.

SCHMIDT, W., *Totemismus in Afrika*, Freiburg, 1955.

SCHWAB, G., *Tribes of the Liberian Hinterland*, Peabody Museum, Cambridge, Mass., 1947.

SEGY, L., 'The Mask in African Dance', *Bulletin of Negro History*, vol. 14, no. 5, Washington D.C. 1953.

SEGY, L., 'Initiation Ceremony and African Sculpture', *American Image*, vol. 10, no. I. French translation *Psyche*, Paris, no. 86, 1953.

SEGY, L., 'Circle-Dot symbolic Sign on African Ivory Carvings', *Zaïre*, vol. vii, no. I, 1953.

SEGY, L., 'African Phallic Symbolism', *Zaïre*, Brussels, 1954.

SEGY, L., 'African Snake Symbolism', *Archiv für Völkerkunde*, Band ix, Vienna, 1954.

SEGY, L., 'L'attitude de l'Africain à l'égard de la maladie. Ses rapports avec la sculpture', *Revue de Psychologie des peuples*, Paris, 1956.

SELIGMAN, C. G., *Les Races de l'Afrique*, Paris, 1935. English edition, Oxford, 1957.

SERGI, G., *Africa, antropologia della stirpe camitica*, Turin, 1897.

SHAW, T., *The Study of Africa's Past*, London, 1946.

SICARD (von), H., 'Ngoma Lungundu—eine afrikanische Bundeslade, *Studia Ethnographica Upsaliensia*, Vol. v, Upsala 1952.

SMITH, E. W., *African Ideas of God*, London, 1950.

SNELGRAVE, W., *Nouvelle relation de quelques endroits de Guinée, et du commerce d'esclaves qu'on y fait*, Amsterdam, 1735.

SOSSOUHOUNTO, F., 'Les anciens rois de la dynastie d'Abomey', *Études Dahoméennes*', 13, Dahomey, 1955.

SOUSBERGHE (de) L., *Structures de parenté et d'alliance d'après les formules Pende, ba-Pende, Congo Belge*, Brussels, 1955.

SPENCER TRIMINGHAM, J., *Islam in the Sudan*, Oxford, 1949.

STANLEY, H. M., *Coomassie and Magdala*, London, 1874.

STANLEY, H. M., *Through the Dark Continent*, Hamburg, 1878. London, 1878.

STAPPERS, L., 'Iets over de Ntambwe Fetisj in Kasai', *Aequatoria*, Coquilhatville, xiv, 1951.

Bibliography

STRAUBE, H., *Die Tierverkleidungen der afrikanischen Naturvölker*, Wiesbaden, 1955.

STUHLMANN, F., *Mit Emin Pacha ins Herz von Afrika*, Leipzig, 1894.

SYDOW (von), E., *Ahnenkult und Ahnenbild der Naturvölker*, Berlin, 1924.

SYDOW (von) E., 'Sbirha Han Coray-e', *Volné smèry*, no. 2. Prague, 1933.

TALBOT, A. P., *In the shadow of the Bush*, London, 1912.

TALBOT, A. P., *The Peoples of Southern Nigeria*, 3 vols., Oxford, 1926.

TAUXIER, L., *Le Noir du Soudan et Études Soudanaises*, 7 vols., Paris, 1912-32.

TAUXIER, L., *Religion, moeurs et coutumes des Agnis de la Côte d'Ivoire*, Paris, 1932.

TAUXIER, L., 'Les Gouin et les Tourouka', *Journal de la société des Africanistes*, 3, Paris, 1933.

TEGNAEUS, H., *La Fraternité de sang. Etude ethno-sociologique des rites de la fraternité de sang notamment en Afrique*, Paris, 1954.

TEMPELS, P., *Bantu philosophy*, Paris, 1949.

THOROBURN, J. W. A., 'The City of Benin', *Nigeria*, no. 10, Lagos, 1937.

TIARKO FOURCHE, J. A. and MORLINGHEM, H., *Les communications des indigènes du Kasai avec les âmes des morts*, Brussels, 1939.

TOOKE, W. D., 'The Initiation of a Baca Isangoma Diviner', *African Studies*, Johannesburg, 14, 1955.

TORDAY, E. and JOYCE, T. A., 'Notes ethnographiques sur les peuples communément appelés Bakuba ainsi que sur les peuples apparentés, les Bushongo', *Annales du Musiée Royal de l'Afrique Centrale*, Brussels, 1911.

TORDAY, E. and JOYCE, T. A., 'Notes ethnographiques sur les peuplades habitant les bassins du Kasai et du Kwango oriental', *Annales du Musée Royal de l'Afrique Centrale. Ethnographie-Anthropologie*, Série 3, Tome 2, Fasc. 1. Brussels, 1922.

TORDAY, E., 'The Influence of the Kingdom of Kongo in Central Africa', *Africa*, London, April, 1928.

TUCKER, J. T., *Angola, The land of the Blacksmith Prince*, London, 1933.

Bibliography

TUCKER, J. T., 'Initiation Ceremonies for Luimbi Boys', *Africa*, January, 1949.

URVOY, Y., 'Histoire des Pays du Soudan Central', *Bulletin du Comité d'études historiques et scientifiques de l'A.O.F.*, Paris, 1936.

VANSINA, J., *Les Tribus Ba-Kuba et les Peuplades apparentées*, Tervueren, 1954.

VANSINA, J., 'Les valeurs culturelles des Bushong', *Zaïre*, 8, Brussels, 1954.

VANSINA, J., 'Initiation Rituals of the Bushong', *Africa*, 25, London, 1955.

VERGIAT, A. M., *Les rites secrets des Primitifs de l'Oubangui*, Paris, 1951.

VERLY, R., 'Le "Roi divin" chex les Ovimbundu et les Kimbundu de l'Angola', *Zaïre*, 9, Brussels, 1955.

VERNEAU, R., 'Les Fétiches à travers les âges', *La Nature*, Paris, April, 1925.

WADSTROM, C. B., *Précis sur l'établissement des Colonies de Sierra Leone et de Boulama*, Paris, 1798.

WAINWRIGHT, G. A., 'Pharaonic Survivals between Lake Tchad and the West Coast', *Journal of Egyptian Archaeology*, 35, London, 1949.

WEEKS, J. H., *Among the Primitive Bakongo*, Philadelphia, 1914.

WESTERMANN, D., *Les Peuples et les Civilisations de l'Afrique*, Paris, 1948.

WESTERMANN, D., *Geschichte Afrikas*, Cologne, 1952.

WESTERMARCK, E., 'Negro Influence in Morocco', *Negro*, ed. N. Cunard, London, 1934.

WEULERSSE, J., *L'Afrique Noire*, Paris, 1934.

WIESCHHOFF, H., *Die Ruinen von Simbabwe u. die süderythräische Kultur*, Bilderbuchblatt 5, Mittel. des Forschungs-Inst. f. Kulturmorpholog., Frankfurt-am-Main, 1934.

WIESCHOFF, H. A., *Africa*, Philadelphia, 1945.

WILSON, J. L., *Western Africa; Its History, Condition and Prospects*, London, 1856.

WOODSON, C. G., *African Heroes and Heroines*, Washington, 1944.

WOODSON, C. G., *African Myth*, Washington, 1944.

ZELTNER (de), F., 'La confrérie des N'tomon en Afrique Occidentale. Le culte du Nama au Soudan, *Bulletin de la Société d'Anthropologie de Paris*, 6th series, vol. I, Paris, 1912.

Bibliography

ZOLINER, H., *Das Togoland und die Sklavenküste*, Berlin, 1855.

ZUCCHELLI, A., *Relazione del viaggio e missione del Congo*, Venice, 1712.

ART

ADAM, L., *Primitive Art*, London, 1940.

Afrikansk Negerkunst Og-Kunsthaandvaerk, Katalog over en Samling, Copenhagen, April, 1946.

Afrikaanske Kunst in Nederland, Leiden, 1947.

Ars Exotica, Catal., Gand (Belgium), 1950.

L'Art Nègre, Présence Africaine, nos. 10-11, Paris, 1951.

L'Art Nègre du Congo Belge, Brussels, 1950.

Arte Negra, Exhibition organised by A. von Hoerschelmann, 'Il Collezionista', Milan, November, 1952.

BALANDIER, G., 'Les conditions sociologiques de l'Art Noir', *L'Art Nègre*, Paris, 1951.

BASLER, A., *L'Art chez les Peuples primitifs*, Paris, 1929.

BOAS, F., *Primitive Art*, Oslo, London, Cambridge, 1927.

CARRIERI, R., *Introductivo catalogo della Mostra d'Arte Negra*, Galleria del Naviglio, Milan, October, 1959.

CASSON, S., 'Negro Art', *The Listener*, London, May 1933.

CHAUVET, S., *Les Arts indigènes des colonies Françaises*, Paris, 1924.

CLOUZOT, H. and LEVEL, A., *L'Art du Congo Belge*, Paris, 1921.

CULIN, S., *Primitive Negro Art*, Brooklyn Museum, 1923.

DARK, PH. J. C., *Bush Negro Art*, London, 1954.

DELAFOSSE, M., 'L'Art ancien dans l'Afrique occidentale', *Renaissance de l'Art Français*, Paris, April 1922.

ECKSTEIN, H., 'Afrikanische Negerkunst', *Kunst und Künstler*, Berlin. (No date.)

EINSTEIN, C., *Exotismes. Exposition au Portique*, Paris, 1925.

EINSTEIN, C., 'A propos de l'exposition de la Galerie Pigalle', *Documents*, no. 2, Paris, 1930.

FAGG, W., 'L'Art Nigérien avant Jésus-Christ, *L'Art Nègre*, Paris, 1951.

FAGG, W., 'De l'Art des Yoruba', *L'Art Nègre, Présence Africaine*, Paris, 1951.

FAGG, W., 'Observations on Nigerian Art History', in *Masterpieces of African Art*, Brooklyn Museum, New York, 1954.

FARNHAM, DORSET. General handbook to the Pitt-Rivers Museum, Farnham, Dorset.

Bibliography

FREYBERG, H., 'Urwaldkunst in Angola', *Weltkunst*, Berlin, 1929.

FROBENIUS, L., 'L'Art africain', *Cahiers d'Art*, 5, nos. 8-9.

FROBENIUS, L., 'Alte und junge afrikanische Kunst', *Die Kunstwelt*, 2, 1912.

FRY, R., *Vision and Design*, London, 1920.

GAFFE, R., *La sculpture au Congo Belge*, Brussels, 1945.

GRIAULE, M., 'Art et Symbole en Afrique Noire', *L'Art Nègre*, *Présence Afrique*, Paris, 1951.

GRIAULE, M., *Art de l'Afrique Noire*, Paris, 1947.

GRIAULE, M., *Folk Art of Black Africa*, New York, 1950.

GRIAULE, M., 'Les symboles des Arts Africaines', *L'Art Nègre Présence Africaine*, Paris, 1951.

GRIAULE, M., 'Art et Symbole en Afrique Noire', *L'Art Nègre Presence Africaine*, Paris, 1951.

GLÜCK, J. F., *Die Kunst Neger-Afrikas*, Stuttgart, 1956.

GOLUBEW, V., *L'Art nègre*, Paris (no date).

GORER, G., 'Black Art', *The Listener*, London, August, 1935.

HARDY, G., *L'Art Nègre. L'Art Animiste des Noirs d'Afrique*, Paris, 1927.

HAUSENSTEIN, W., *Barbaren und Klassiker. Ein Buch von der Bildnerei exotischer Völker*, Munich, 1922.

HERSKOVITS, M. J., 'The Art of Dahomey', *American Magazine of Art*, vol. xxvii, nos., 2-3, 1934.

HIMMELHEBER, H., *Negerkünstler*, Stuttgart, 1935.

HIMMELHEBER, H., 'Art et Artistes Bakuba', *Brousse*, no. I, Léopoldville, 1940.

HOWLETT, J., 'L'Art Nègre? Connais pas!', *L'Art Nègre*, *Présence Africaine*, Paris, 1951.

KUHN, H., *Die Kunst der Primitiven*, Munich, 1923.

LEBEUF, J.-P, 'L' Art du Delta Chari', *L'Art Nègre*, *Présence Africaine*, 10-11, Paris, 1951.

LECOQ, R., 'Quelques apsects de l'Art Bamoun', *L'Art Nègre*, *Présence Africaine*, 10-11, Paris, 1951.

LEM, F. H., 'Musique et Arts Nègres', *Bulletin de la sociétié des recherches soudanaises*, no. 36, Koulouba, September, 1936.

LEM, F. H., *L'Art de l'Afrique centrale*, Paris, 1950.

LEM, F. H., 'Varieté et unité des traditions plastiques de l'Afrique Noire', *L'Art Nègre*, *Présence Africaine*, 10-11, Paris, 1951.

Le Musée Vivant, Numéro Spéciale, Paris, November, 1948.

Bibliography

LEPAGE, P. C., *La décoration primitive: Afrique*, 1922.

LOCKE, A., 'Collection of Congo Art', *The Arts*, New York, February, 1927.

LOCKE, A., 'Introduction to the Catalogue of the Blondian Theatre of Arts', *Collection of Primitive African Arts*, New York, 1927.

LOCKE, A., 'African Art, Classical Style', *American Magazine of Art*, New York, May 1935.

LOCKE, A., *The Significance of African Art*, Baltimore Museum of Art, 1946.

LONDON: Royal Anthropological Institute: Traditional Art of the British Colonies, London, 1949.

LUQUET, G. H., *L'Art Primitif*, Paris, 1930.

MAES, J., 'La psychologie de l'Art Nègre', *IPEK*, Leipzig, 1926.

MAES, J., (Intro.) *Variétés*, numéro spéciale consacré à l'Art Nègre, no. 7, Brussels, 1928.

MAES, J. and LAVACHERY, H., *L'Art Nègre à l'Exposition du Palais des Beaux-Arts*, Brussels-Paris, 1930.

MAES, J., 'Des sources de l'Art Nègre', *Cahiers d'Art*, no. 6, Paris, 1930.

MAQUET, M., 'Contribution à l'étude des crucifix anciens indigènes du Bas-Congo', *Arts et métiers indigènes de la Province de Léopoldville*, no. 6, March 1938.

MAURICE, H., 'A propos d'art Ba-Luba', *Revue d'Ethnographie et des traditions populaires*, Paris, 1920.

MEDGYES, L., 'Art of African Negro', *International Studio*, vol. 70, New York, November, 1922.

MURRAY, K. C., 'Nigeria's First Exhibition of Antiquities', *Nigeria*, no. 26, Lagos, 1947.

Negerkonst, Nationalmuseum, Stockholm, March-April, 1953.

OLBRECHTS, F. M., 'Contribution to the Study of the Chronology of African Plastic Art', *Africa*, London, October, 1945.

OLIVEIRA (de), J. O., *El Arte Negro*, Madrid, 1956.

PAUVERT, J. CL., 'Approche de l'Art Africain noir', *L'Art Nègre, Présence Africaine*, Paris, 1951.

PAUWELS, M., 'Les couleurs et les dessins au Ruanda', *Anthropos*, xlvii, 1952.

PERIER, G. D., 'L'Art des Noirs. Que doit-on penser et espérer de la peinture congolaise?', *Congo-Tervueren*, I, Tervueren, 1955.

Bibliography

PERIER, G. D., *Les Arts Populaires du Congo Belge*, Brussels, 1948.

PESCHUEL-LOESCHE, E., *Völkerkunde von Loango*, Stuttgart, 1907.

PORTIER, A. and PONCETTON, F., *Les Arts Sauvages d'Afrique*, Paris, 1929.

Primitive Art, University of Minnesota, 1940.

ROUQUET, A. 'L'Art Nègre', *Le Domain colonial français*, vol. iv, 1930.

SADLER, M. E., *Arts of West Africa*, Oxford, 1935.

SALMON, A., 'Negro Art', *The Burlington Magazine*, London, 1920.

SALMON, A., *L'Art Nègre*, Paris, 1922.

SCHMALENBACH, W., *African Art*, New York, 1954.

SCHWEINFURTH, G., *Artes Africanae*, Leipzig, London, 1875.

SEGY (Szecsi), L., 'The Term "Negro Art" is essentially a non-African Concept', *Negro*, ed. N. Cunard, London, 1934.

SEGY, L., 'Towards a New Historical Concept of Negro Africa', *The Journal of Negro History*, vol. 38, no. 1, Washington, D.C., 1953.

SEGY, L., 'Divers aspects de l'étude de l'Art Africain', *Revue de psychologie des peuples*, 2 trim., 1954.

SEGY, L., 'Liberian Art. A documentation for a cultural heritage for the Liberian People, *Liberia Today*, Washington, D.C., August, 1955.

SEGY, L., *African Art Studies*, New York, 1956.

SEGY, L., 'The Significance of African Art', *Présence Africaine*, vol. xiv, no. 15, June-September, 1957.

SHADBOLT, D., 'Our Relation to Primitive Art', *Canadian Art*, vol. v, no. I, Ottawa, 1947.

SONOLET, L., 'L'Art dans l'Afrique Occidentale Française', *Gazette des Beaux Arts*, Paris, July-December, 1923.

STEPHAN, E., *Südseekunst*, Berlin, 1907.

SWEENEY, J. J., *African Negro Art*, Museum of Modern Art, New York, 1935.

SYDOW (von), E., *Exotische Kunst, Africa und Oceanien*, Leipzig, 1921.

SYDOW (von), E., *Die Kunst der Naturvölker und der Vorzeit*, Berlin, 1923.

SYDOW (von), E., *Kunst und Religion der Naturvölker*, Oldenburg, 1926.

Bibliography

TATA NSIESIE, 'Notes sur les Christs et Statues de l'ancien Congo', *Brousse*, no. 3, Léopoldville, 1939.

VATICAN CITY: Vatican Exhibition, *The Arts in the Belgian Congo and Ruanda-Urundi*, Brussels, 1950.

WINGERT, P. S., 'Congo Art', *Transactions*, University Museum, New York, 1947.

WINGERT, P. S., *African Negro Sculpture*, San Francisco, 1948.

ZAYAS (de), M., *African Negro Art*, New York, 1916.

ZERVOS, C., 'Art Nègre', *Cahiers d'Art*, nos. 7-8, Paris, 1927.

SCULPTURES IN WOOD AND IVORY

AFRIKANISCHE PLASTIK, *Kunst Werk Schrift.*, vol. xvii, Baden-Baden, 1952.

ANDRÉE, R., 'Alte Westafrikanische Elfenbeinschnitzwerke im Herzog Anton Ulrich-Museum zu Braunschweig', *Globus*, no. 79, Braunschweig, 1901.

ANTI, C., 'Scultura negra', *Dedalo*, 1921.

BOSSCHE (Van den), A. 'La sculpture des masques Bapende', *Brousse*, no. 1, Léopoldville, 1950.

BOSSCHE (Van den), J., 'L'Art plastique chez les Bapende', *Brousse*, no. 2, Léopoldville, 1950.

BUREAUD, G., *Les Masques*, Paris, 1948.

CLOUZOT, H. and LEVEL, A., *Sculptures Africaines et Océaniennes*, Paris (no date—1923?).

EBERL-ELBER, R., 'Die Masken der Männerbünde in Sierra Leone', *Ethnos*, no. 2, Stockholm, 1937.

EINSTEIN, C., *Negerplastik*, Munich, 1920. Italian edition, *Scultura Africana*, Rome (no date).

EINSTEIN, C., *Afrikanische Plastik*, Berlin, 1921.

ESSWEIN, H., 'Masken', *Frankfurter Zeitung*, 3 May, 1933.

FAGG, W., *The Sculpture of Africa*, London, 1948.

FRIEND, D., 'Masks', *Nigeria*, no. 18, Lagos, 1939.

FROBENIUS, L., *Die Masken und Geheimbünde Afrikas*, Leipzig, 1898.

GAFFE, R., *La Sculpture au Congo Belge*, Paris-Brussels, 1945.

GERMANN, P., 'Das plastich-figürliche Kunstgewerbe im Grasland', *Jahrbuch des stadtischen Museums für Völkerkunde*, no. iv, Leipzig, 1910.

GREGOR, J., *Die Masken der Erde*, Munich, 1936.

GRIAULE, M., *Masques Dogon*, Paris, 1938.

Bibliography

GUILLAUME, P. and MONRO, T., *Primitive Negro Sculpture*, London-New York, 1926.

HALL, H. U., *Two Masks from French Equatorial Africa*, University of Pennsylvania, Philadelphia, December, 1947.

HEGER, F., *Alte Elfenbeinarbeiten aus Afrika in den Wiener Sammlungen*, Vienna, 1899.

HEYDRICH, M. and FRÖLICH, W., *Plastik der Primitiven*, Stuttgart, 1954.

HUNT-COOKE, A. and MURRAY, K. C., 'Dahomeyan Craft', *Nigeria*, no. 10, Lagos, 1937.

JEFFREYS, M. D. W., 'Altars or Sacred Stools: The Ibo "Tazza" or "Ada" ', *Man*, 42-60, London, 1955.

KARUTZ, R., 'Die afrikanischen Hoernermasken', *Mitteilungen der Geographischen Gesellschaft* Lübeck, 1901.

KEIMER, L., A propos des coussins des anciens Égyptiens et des Bedjas modernes', *Bulletin de l'Institut d'Egypte*, 37, 1956 (see also BIE xxx).

KJERSMEIER, C., 'Bambara Sculpture', *Negro Anthology*, ed. N. Cunard, London, 1934.

KJERSMEIER, C., *Centres de style de la Sculpture Nègre Africaine*, 4 vols., Paris, 1935-38.

KJERSMEIER, C., *Afrikanske Negerskulpturer—African Negro Sculptures*, Copenhagen, 1947.

KJERSMEIER, C., *Scultura Africana* (translated by G. Prampolini), Scheiwiller, Milan, 1959.

KOCHNITZKY, L., *African Negro Sculptures*, New York, 1948.

LAVACHERY, H., 'Essay on the Styles in Statuary of the Belgian Congo', *Negro*, ed. N. Cunard, London, 1934.

LAVACHERY, H., 'Apparente évolution des masques dans la région de Man', *Bulletin des Musées royaux d'Art et d'Histoire*, Brussels, November-December, 1939.

LEM, F. H., *Sculptures Soudanaises*, Paris, 1948.

MAES, J., 'Les figurines sculptées du Bas Congo', *Africa*, London, July, 1930.

MAES, J., *Fetischen of Toverbeelden uit Kongo*, Brussels, 1935.

MALRAUX, A., *Le Musée Imaginaire de la Sculpture Mondiale*, Paris, 1952. (Denise Schaeffner was responsible for the African section.)

MASSARI, C., 'Maschere da danza degli Uaboni', *Archivio per l'Antropologia e l'Etnologia*, Florence, 80-81, 1950-1.

Bibliography

MEYEROWITZ, E. L. R., 'Wood-Carving in the Yoruba Country Today', *Africa*, London, April, 1945.

MICHELET, R., 'Eight Drawings of Congo Masks from Tervueren Museum', *Negro Anthology*, ed. N. Cunard, London, 1934.

MUENSTERBERGER, W., *Sculpture of Primitive Man*, London, 1955.

NUOFFER, O., *Afrikanische Plastik und die Gestaltung von Mutter und Kind*, Dresden, 1934.

OLBRECHTS, F. M., *Plastiek van Kongo*, Brussels, 1946.

OLBRECHTS, F. M., 'Découverte de deux statuettes d'un grand sous-style Ba-Luba', *Bulletin Institut royal coloniale Belge*, 22, Brussels, 1951.

PEISSI, P., 'Les masques blancs des tribus de l'Ogoue', *L'Art Nègre Présence Africaine*, 10-11, Paris, 1951.

RADIN, P. and SWEENEY, J. J., *African Folktales and Sculpture*, Bollingen Series, No. xxxiii, New York, 1953.

RATTON, C., *Masques Africains*, Paris, 1931.

SCHNEIDER-LENGYEL, L., *Die Welt der Maske*, Munich, 1934.

SEGY, L., 'Warega Ivories', *Zaïre*, Brussels, December, 1951.

SEGY, L., 'Bakota Funerary Figures', *Zaïre*, Brussels, vol. vi, no. 5, 1952.

SEGY, L., 'African Sculpture and Writing', *The Journal of Human Relations*, Wilberforce, Ohio, December, 1952.

SEGY, L., 'Bakuba Cups: An Essay on Style-Classification', *Midwest Journal*, vol. iv, no. 1, Winter 1951-52, Jefferson City.

SEGY, L., *African Sculpture Speaks*, New York, 1952 (2nd ed. 1955).

SEGY, L., 'African Names and Sculpture', *Acta Tropica*, vol. 10, no. 4, Basle, 1953.

SEGY, L., African Sculpture and Animism', *The Journal of Human Relations*, vol. 2, no. 1, Wilberforce, 1953.

SEGY, L., 'Shango Sculptures', *Acta Tropica*, vol. 12, no. 2, Basle, 1955.

SEGY, L., 'The Artistic Quality of African Sculpture', *Tribus*, Band 6, Stuttgart, 1957.

SEGY, L., *African Sculpture*, New York, 1958.

SEGY, L., 'Plastic Aspects of African Sculpture: The Theory of Tension', *Review of General Semantic*, vol. xiv, no. 3, 1957.

SEGY, L., *Afrikanische Masken*, Arhbeck (Germania).

SYDOW (von), E., 'African Sculpture', *Africa*, London, April, 1928.

Bibliography

SYDOW (von), E., *Handbuch der Afrikanischen Plastik*, Berlin, 1930.

SYDOW (von), E., *Masques Janus de Cross River*, 'Documents', no. 6, Paris, 1930.

SYDOW (von), E., 'The Image of Janus in African Sculpture', *Africa*, London, January, 1932.

Traditional Sculptures from the Colonies, Colonial Office, London, 1951.

TROWELL, M., *Classical African Sculpture*, London, 1953; New York, 1954.

UNDERWOOD, L., *Figures in Wood of West Africa*, London, 1947.

UNDERWOOD, L., *Masks of West Africa*, London, 1948.

UNDERWOOD, L., *Bronzes of West Africa*, London, 1949.

UTZINGER, R., *Masken*, Berlin, 1922.

VANDENHOUTE, P. J. L., *Classification Stylistique du Masque Dan et Guere de la Côte d'Ivoire Occidentale* (A.O.F.) Mededelingen Rijksmuseum voor Volkenkunde, No. 4, Leiden, 1948.

VATTER, E., *Religiöse Plastik der Naturvölker*, Frankfurt-on-Main, 1926.

WEYNS, J., 'Quelques remarques au sujet de nos Sculptures Africaines', *Les Arts Plastiques*, Brussels, 1948.

WINGERT, P. S., *The Sculpture of Negro Africa*, New York 1950.

WINGERT, P. S., 'Anatomical Interpretations in African Masks', *Man*, 100-125, 1954.

METAL, STONE, TERRACOTTAS

BALFOUR, H., 'The Thunderbolt Celts from Benin', *Man*, no. 3, London, 1903.

BALFOUR, H., 'Modern Brass-casting in West Africa', *Journal of the Royal Anthropological Institute*, vol. 40, 1910.

BARDON, P., 'Catalogue de la Collection des Masques d'or Baoulé,' *Institut Français d'Afrique Noire*, Dakar, 1948.

BLAHA, H., 'Eine wenig beobachtete Kunstfertigkeit der afrikanischen Neger: Skulpturen aus Lehm und Ton', *Wiener völkerkund. Mitteilungen*, 1, 1954.

BOULTON, L. C., *Bronze Artists of West Africa*, New York, 1934.

CHAUVET, S., 'Objets d'or, de bronze et d'ivoire dans l'Art nègre', *Cahiers d'Art*, no. I, Paris, 1930.

CLARKE, J. D., 'The Stone Figures of Esie', *Nigeria*, no. 14, Lagos, 1938.

Bibliography

CLINE, W., *Mining and Metallurgy in Negro Africa*, Menasha, Wis. (USA), 1937.

D'ARCORE, M., 'Gli "antenati" di Esie', *Le Vie del Mondo*, August, 1942.

DELAFOSSE, M., 'Au sujet des statuettes en pierre de Kissi', *Revue d'Ethnographie et de Sociologie*, Paris, 1914.

DUCKWORTH, E. H., 'Recent archaeological discoveries in the ancient city of Ifé', *Nigeria*, no. 14, Lagos, 1938.

EGHAREVBA, J. V., 'Art and Craft Works in the City of Benin', *Nigeria*, no. 18, 1939.

'Exp. Bronzes et Ivoires de Bénin au Palais de Trocadero' (Preface by C. Ratton), *Cahiers d'Art*, Paris, 1932. (Catalogue.)

FAGG, B., 'Pottery Figures from Northern Nigeria', *Africa*, London, January, 1945.

FAGG, W., 'The Antiquities of Ifé', *Magazine of Art*, New York, April, 1950.

FAGG, W., 'The Allman Collection of Benin Antiquities', *Man*, no. 261, London, 1953.

FROBENIUS, L., 'Terrakotten aus Ifé', *Feuer*, 3, Weimar, 1921.

GASKELL, W., 'The Influence of Europe on early Benin Art', *The Connoisseur*, London, June, 1902.

HAGEN, K., *Altertümer von Benin Hamburgischen Museum für Völkerkunde zu Hamburg*, Hamburg, 1898.

HEFEL, A., 'Der Afrikanische Gelbguss und seine Beziehung zu dtn Mittelmeerlaendern', *Wiener Beiträge*, Jahr. 5, Vienna, 1943.

HEFEL, A., *Afrikanische Bronzen*, Vienna, 1948.

HOOTON, E. A., *Benin Antiquities in the Peabody Museum*, Cambridge, Mass., 1917, *Varia Africana I.*

KJERSMEIER, C., *Ashanti-Vaegtlodder*, Copenhagen, 1948. English edition: *Ashanti Weights*, by the same publisher. Italian edition: *Pesi degli Ashanti*, Scheiwiller, Milan, 1953.

LUSCHAN (von), F., 'Die Karl Knorrsche Sammlung von Benin', *Altertümerie in Museum für Lander and Völkerkunde*, Stuttgart, 1901.

LUSCHAN (von), F., *Die Altertümer von Benin*, 3 vols., Berlin, 1919.

MARQUART, J., *Die Benin-Sammlung des Reichsmuseums für Völkerkunde in Leiden*, Leiden, 1913.

MEYEROWITZ, E., 'Bronzes and Terra-Cottas from Ile-Ifé', *The Burlington Magazine*, London, October, 1939.

Bibliography

MEYEROWITZ, E., 'Ancient Nigerian Bronzes', *The Burlington Magazine*, London, September-October, 1941.

MEYEROWITZ, E., 'The Stone Figures of Esie in Nigeria', *The Burlington Magazine*, London, February, 1943.

PALMER, R., 'Ancient Nigerian Bronzes', *The Burlington Magazine*, London, October, 1942.

PAULME, D., 'A Propos des Kuduo Ashanti', *L'Art Nègre Présence Africaine*, 10-11, Paris, 1951.

PITT-RIVERS (Lt.-Gen.), *Antique Works of Art from Benin*, London, 1900.

RATTON, C., 'The Ancient Bronzes of Black Africa', *Negro Anthology*, ed. N. Cunard, London, 1934.

RATTON, C., 'L'or fétiche', *L'Art Nègre, Présence Africaine*, 10-11, Paris, 1951.

READ, C. H. and DALTON, O. M., *Antiquities from the City of Benin and from other parts of West Africa in the British Museum*, London, 1899.

ROTH, H. LING, 'Primitive Art from Benin', *Studio*, London, October, 1898.

STRUCK, B., 'Die Chronologie der Benin Altertümer, *Zeitschrift für Ethnologie*, vol. I, lv, 1923.

SYDOW (von), E., 'Ancient and Modern Art in Benin City', *Africa*, London, January, 1938.

UNDERWOOD, L., *Bronzes of West Africa*, London, 1949.

WEBSTER PLASS (Madame), 'Poids à or Ashant', *L'Art Nègre Présence Africaine*, 10-11, Paris, 1951.

ZELLER, R., 'Die Goldgewichte von Ashante', *Baessler Archiv*, III, Leipzig, 1912.

NEGRO ART AND MODERN ART
(Comparative Material)

ADÉMA, M., *Guillaume Apollinaire le mal-aimé*, Paris, 1952.

APOLLINAIRE, G., *Sculptures nègres* (Preface by Paul Guillaume), Paris, 1917.

BARNES, A., 'Primitive Negro Sculpture and its influence in modern civilization', *Opportunity*, New York, May, 1928.

BARR, A. H., *Picasso, Fifty Years of his Art*, New York, 1956.

BELL, C., *Since Cézanne*, London, 1922.

BRETON, A., 'Sur le Précubisme de Picasso', *Formes*, no. 4, Paris, 1931.

Bibliography

BUFFET-PICABIA, G., *Aires Abstraites*, Geneva, 1957.

CARDNUFF RITCHIE, A., *Sculpture of the Twentieth Century*, New York (no date).

CARRIERI, R., *Pittura Scultura d'avanguardia (1890-1950) in Italia*, Milan, 1950.

CENDRARS, B., *Anthologie Nègre*, Paris, 1927.

CENDRARS, B., *Comment les Blancs sont d'anciens Noirs*, Paris, 1942.

CENDRARS, B., *Petits Contes nègres pour les enfants des blancs*, Paris, 1943.

DIEHL, G., *H. Matisse*, Paris, 1954.

GAUGUIN, P., *Noa, Noa, Voyage de Tahiti*, Stockholm, 1947.

GIEDION-WELCKER, C., *Moderne Plastik*, Zürich, 1937.

GOLDWATER, R. J., *Primitivism in Modern Painting*, New York, 1938.

GRAHAM, J. D., 'Primitive Art and Picasso', *Magazine of Art*, April, 1937.

KAHNWEILER, D. H., 'Negro Art and Cubism', *Horizon*, London, December, 1948. See *Présence Africaine*, Paris, no. 3, 1948.

KUHN, A., *Die Neuere Plastik*, Munich, 1922.

LEWIS, D., *Brancusi*, London, 1957.

'Matisse (H.)' by C. Zervos, P. Fierens, P. Guéguen, G. Salles, R. Fry, H. McBride, W. Grohmann, K. Asplund, G. Scheiwiller, G. Apollinaire, *Cahiers d'Art*, Paris, 1931.

MODIGLIANI, J., *Modigliani senza leggenda*, Florence, 1958.

'Opinions sur l'Art Nègre', by G. Apollinaire, J. Cocteau, J. Gris, P. Guillaume, J. Lipchitz, P. Picasso, M. Vlaminck, *Action*, Paris, April, 1920.

POUND, E., *Gaudier-Brzeska*, London, 1916.

POUND, E., 'Brancusi', *The Little Review*, Autumn, 1921.

POUND, E., *Brancusi*; translated by M. de Rachewiltz, Scheiwiller, Milan, 1957.

SAVINIO, A., *Souvenirs*, Rome, 1945.

TZARA, T., 'La Sculpture africaine et l'Art moderne', *Konstrevy*, no. 2, Stockholm, 1933.

VALENTINER, W. R., *Origins of Modern Sculpture*, New York, 1946.

VLAMINCK, M., *Portraits avant Décès*, Paris, 1943.

ZERVOS, C., *Histoire de l'Art Contemporain: Influence de l'Art Nègre*, Paris, 1938.

Bibliography

ZERVOS, C., *Pablo Picasso* (see vol. 2, 1912-17), Paris, 1942.

ZERVOS, C., 'Constantin Brancusi', *Cahiers d'Art*, Paris, 1957.

PRESENT AND FUTURE

BRAUSCH, B., 'La Crise de l'artisanat rural', *Brousse*, nos. 1-2, Léopoldville, 1949.

'Evidence de la culture nègre', *Le Musée Vivant*, Paris, November, 1948.

FAGG, W., 'Arts anciens et Parodies modernes', *Nature*, I, 22, 1949.

FROBENIUS, L., 'Early African Culture as an Indication of Present Negro Potentialities', *The Annals*, American Academy of Political and Social Science, Philadelphia, 1928, no. 140.

FROBENIUS, L., 'Afrika in Hundert Jahren', *Die Woche*, 18 March 1933.

GREBERT, F., 'Arts en voie de disparition au Gabon', *Africa*, London, January, 1934.

GUILLET, C., 'La rénovation des métiers indigènes au Soudan Français', *Bulletin de la Sociéte des recherches Soudanaises*, no. 36, Koulouba, September, 1936.

ITALIAANDER, W., *Neue Kunst in Afrika*, Mannheim, 1957.

LAVACHERY, H., 'L'art des Noirs d'Afrique et son destin', *L'Art Nègre, Présence Africaine*, 10-11, Paris, 1951.

KUTSCHER, G., 'West-Afrika und die Moderne Kunst', *Bildende Kunst*, Berlin, November-December, 1946.

LEIRIS, M., *Les Nègres d'Afrique et les arts Sculpturaux*, Ed. UNESCO, 1949.

MERCIER, P., 'Evolution de l'Art Dahoméen', *L'Art Nègre, Présence Africaine*, 10-11, Paris, 1951.

MURRAY, K. C., 'Arts and Crafts of Nigeria: Their Past and Future', *Africa*, London, October, 1945.

SCOHY, A., 'Réflexions sur l'évolution de l'Art congolais', *Brousse*, nos. 1-2, Léopoldville, 1948.

SEGY, L., 'Future of African Art, *Midwest Journal*, Lincoln University, Summer, 1952.

STEVENS, G. A., 'The Future of African Art', *Africa*, London, April, 1930.

Bibliography

BY THE AUTHOR

Massime degli antichi Egiziani. Scheiwiller, Milano: 1959
Liriche amorose degli antichi Egiziani. Scheiwiller, Milano: 1959
Scarabei dell'antico Egitto. Scheiwiller, Milano: 1957
Incantesimi e scongiuri degli antichi Exiziani. Scheiwiller, Milano: 1958
Incontro con l'Arte Egiziana. Martello, Milano: 1958*
Vita nell'antico Egitto. Sansoni, Firenze: 1958
Il Libro dei Morti degli antichi Egiziani. Scheiwiller, Milano: 1958
Il Libro Egizio degli Inferi. Atanor, Roma: 1959
Incontro con l'Arte Africana. Martello, Milano: 1959*
The Rock-Tomb of Irw-K3-Pth, Monumenta et Documenta Orientis Antiqui. Brill, Leiden: 1960.
I Miti e Luoghi dell'antico Egitto. Longanesi, Milano: 1961
Egitto magico-religioso. Boringhieri, Torino: 1961
Testi e simboli magici egiziani. Scheiwiller, Milano: 1962
Eros Nero: Milano: Longanesi & C. 1964†

PUBLICATIONS IN PRESS

Atlante d'Arte Africana. Longanesi, Milano
Amuleti dell'antico Egitto: Scheiwiller, Milano
Il Manuale dell'Archeologo. Longanesi, Milano
Il Libro delle Due Vie. Boringhieri, Torino

*Translations have variously appeared in English and Danish.
†Translations in English, French, German, Spanish.

INDEX

Index

Index

Index

Index

Index

Index

Index

Spiritain, Father, 86
Stanleyville, 123
Stockholm, Ollers Collection, Pl. 36
Stracmans, 46
Sudan, former Anglo-Egyptian, 15, 26, 61, 86, 90, 123; Pl. 65
Sudan, Eastern, 41
Sudan, French, 7-8, 91, 94, 145; Pl. 31
Sumanguru, 36, 39
Sun (cult), 48
Sundiata, 39, 40
Switzerland, 1
Sydow, E. von, 110

Tada, 65
Tago, 75
Tagzelt, 20; Pl. A
Tahiti, 153
Talbot, P. A., 62
Tanganyika, 15, 27, 123; Pl. 66
Tapa, 72, 143
Tarikh-el-Fettach, 35, 37
Tarikh-es-Sudan, 35, 37
Tassili, 15, 21, 22
Tate Gallery, 84
Tekrur, 42
Tel Issaghen, 17
Tell el Amarna, 51
Tibesti, 15
Tikenu, 22
Timbuktu, 34, 37, 40, 41
Tjiwara, 92
Togo, 10, 12
Transvaal, 15
Tuareg, 19
tukula (powder), 118

Uan Amil, 20
Uan Muhugiag, 20
Ubanghi-Shari, 47, 76
Umtali, Pl. 5
Underwood, 86
Un-nofre, 45

Vallisnieri, 126
Venturi, Lionello, 145
Venus (morning star), 28
Versailles, 138

Vienna, 66
Vlaminck, Maurice, 139-40, 142, 143

Wabembe, 115
Wadai, 44
Wadiri, L., xvii, 154-5; Pl. 87
Wagadugu, 38
Wagogo, 8
Walata, 37
Wallace Collection, xvii, xviii; Pl. 72
Walrond, E., xvii
Wamba, 56
Wango, 94
Wara, 93
Warega, 8, 44, 90, 115, 123, 125; Pl. F, 68
Wasu, 50
Watschiwokwe, 125 n. *See* Batshioko
Winkler, H. A., 23
Wolof, 40, 42

Yabassi, 32
Yagua, 27
Yakoba, 97
Yalnas, 8
Ya-mama, 97
Yassi (secret society), 97
Yatenga, 38, 39
Yemaja (divinity), 100
Yodola, 95
Yolo (secret association), 118
Yoruba, 34, 42, 57, 58, 60, 61, 62, 63, 71, 72, 73, 77, 84, 100, 101, 102-3, 106, 132; Pl. 9, 10, 43, 44
Yucatan, 122

Za, the, 36
Zado, the, 154
Zambesi (river), 1, 28, 127
Zanzibar, 41
Zerries, Dr O., xvii
Zervos, 142, 143
Zimbabwe, 28 et seq., 48, 77-8 Pl. 29
Zuenula, 97
Zulu, 8, 50